M.E. SMITH

W9-AZJ-054

# The Hitchhiker's Guide to Lean

Copyright © 2006 Society of Manufacturing Engineers

987654

All rights reserved, including those of translation. This book, or parts thereof, may not be reproduced by any means, including photocopying, recording or microfilming, or by any information storage and retrieval system, without permission in writing of the copyright owners.

No liability is assumed by the publisher with respect to use of information contained herein. While every precaution has been taken in the preparation of this book, the publisher assumes no responsibility for errors or omissions. Publication of any data in this book does not constitute a recommendation or endorsement of any patent, proprietary right, or product that may be involved.

Library of Congress Catalog Card Number: 2005932553
International Standard Book Number: 0-87263-831-6

*Additional copies may be obtained by contacting:*

Society of Manufacturing Engineers
Customer Service
One SME Drive, P.O. Box 930
Dearborn, Michigan 48121
1-800-733-4763
www.sme.org

*SME staff who participated in producing this book:*

Steve Bollinger, Manager, Book and Video Publications
Rosemary Csizmadia, Senior Production Editor
Frances Kania, Administrative Coordinator
Christine Verdone, Graphic Designer

Printed in the United States of America

# The Hitchhiker's Guide to Lean
## Lessons from the Road

Jamie Flinchbaugh
Andy Carlino

with Foreword by Dennis Pawley

 Society of Manufacturing Engineers
Dearborn, MI

*This book is dedicated to all the hard working men and women who do whatever it takes to move their organization along on the road to the ideal state.*

# Acknowledgments

There are, of course, many more people to whom we owe thanks than we can mention here, not just for their contributions to this book but for their contributions to our learning and our lives.

We would first like to thank our many clients, past and present. The individuals and the companies they work for are too numerous to name, but without them there would be no Lean Learning Center and no *Hitchhiker's Guide to Lean*. We are continually thankful for the challenging and vital questions they ask of us, always pushing us to explore new ground.

We could not serve our clients without a wonderful team, to whom we owe a great debt, and whose dedication to progress and service is without equal.

We also would like to thank the Society of Manufacturing Engineers (SME) for those who helped develop and edit this book and for its dedication to serving the manufacturing community, bringing the state of lean knowledge forward.

Art Levine deserves thanks for his work in polishing the rough edges of this book through its early stages.

Lastly, we would like to thank our families, particularly our wives, for their love and support without which this book would not be possible. Many days are spent away from our families as we serve our clients; returning home to write a book increased the burden.

# Foreword

This book will help you learn lean, taking you through everything from lean principles to pitfalls to avoid. As someone responsible for leading lean, I will share some of my thoughts of what it takes to be successful on this journey.

What is the primary role of a lean leader? This question is asked far too infrequently, and when it is asked, the answers are predictable—and plain wrong. But it is a vital question, as without leadership, lean will never get off the ground. Common replies include setting the vision, establishing priorities, and providing motivation. Wrong, wrong, and wrong. These are important responsibilities, but the essential purpose of a leader is to do one thing: *create change*.

You don't believe me? Imagine if you had a customer or a shareholder attached at your hip for a day or a week. (For a real test, try actually bringing in a customer or shareholder for a true waste walk.) Whether you sell cars, toasters, or financial services, a percentage of the fees you charge covers your salary. The more senior your position—the more leadership you provide—the higher the percentage. Imagine asking your customer or shareholder to identify which of your activities they would be willing to approve. What do you think they would say? Certainly they would toss out all the time you spend reading emails or sitting in meetings. But, just as certainly, they would value one thing: the change you create to make your products or services faster, cheaper, higher-quality or, in some other way, better. Creating change is the only value-added activity a leader provides.

Some of the other activities leaders perform are necessary, and perhaps no leader creates change all of the time. But what percent of your time are you leading versus managing? To be clear about the difference, *managing* maintains the status quo and keeps current reality going. That's important, but it's not leadership. *Leaders* change things, move them forward, and produce different results than they achieved the day before.

To create a lean change, you need to pay attention to where you are and where you are going. Imagine you are driving a racecar. You focus ahead so that you can gage the turns (otherwise you will run into the wall). But you also look behind you, in the rear-view mirror, to see who might be trying to pass you. The drivers in back of you could be more dangerous than those ahead. You also look left-to-right to see who is alongside of you. As a leader, you need to do the same thing for your organization. You must look ahead, anticipate what's coming, and figure out the changes you need to make to succeed there. You must also look in your rear-view mirror and see who is coming after you, because those in the back of the pack are often willing to take greater risks than you. And you must pay attention to those alongside you who may be trying to squeeze by or pass you. A leader is not responsible for the past; a leader bears responsibility for the future, whether it is a day or a decade away.

As part of looking ahead, many companies write a vision statement. Often, this is a new leader's first task. Yet when I ask people to tell me their vision statement, few are able to do it. Some say they have it jotted on a card in their pocket. Because it does not drive action, however, it is not a vision statement. Vision statements created to go on plaques, annual reports, and marketing materials are not living, breathing things. Leaders must embody vision statements, because the statements ultimately do not matter—it is the *change* they bring that truly matters.

When we began Chrysler's transformation in the early 1990s, we created a vision statement that read, "To become the premier automaker in North America by 1996 and in the world by 2000." I stood up in town hall meetings at our plants and delivered the statement to our employees. To my surprise, I got standing ovations. That vision meant something; it created an image that sharply contrasted with the current reality. But as they were leaving, the employees' blank stares communicated a key question: How would we accomplish this? This illustrates another responsibility of a leader. Beyond creating the vision, a leader must also develop the vehicle that will deliver it. That vehicle was lean.

To effectively chart the course, a leader must have a clear grasp of current reality. This means going beyond the numbers. A leader must be able to understand the good, the bad, and the ugly. Let me share a formula I did not create but have used for many years:

$$H \times V \times F > R$$

$H =$ Hatred of the current reality (This first factor used to be $D =$ dissatisfaction, but I believe people have to really hate their current situation. If they did not, why would they take risks?)

$V =$ Vision of the ideal state—organizations need a compelling place to move toward

$F =$ the courage to take the necessary First steps to close the gap, which is often the most difficult step, because it requires commitment to close the gap and bold, powerful actions to make the necessary change.

$R =$ the Resistance to change that exists within an organization

If any factor is missing, organizations will not be able to move forward. And all of the factors are the responsibility of leaders who, again, must add value to their organizations by creating change.

Creating change, particularly the kind discussed in this book, is a war. It is a war to win the minds and hearts of people and lead them where you want them to go. In the war, there are two types of people: those capable of learning and those who are incapable. Those who cannot, or who refuse to learn, have to go. It is the leader's job to make the call. Remember, all wars have casualties.

While change is a leader's primary role, it is also his or her responsibility to teach. Teaching is the pathway to change.

People who cannot teach, cannot lead. The lean leader must be able to change the way people think through education, coaching, and example. The lean leader must become the walking, talking embodiment of what is being taught.

Without a good leader, nothing changes. If a lean program, or any other program for that matter, is failing, it is probably not the fault of the tools. It is failing because of lousy leadership. As you embark on your lean journey, learn all you can about the concepts, practices, principles, and tools of lean. But remember, above all, the goal of lean is change—and change hinges on your ability to lead. So get out there and lead!

Dennis Pawley
CEO, Pawley Enterprises (Farmington, MI) and
Partner, Lean Learning Center (Novi, MI)

# Introduction

Let us start with a promise: this book is not a repeat of the same lean concepts you have read a dozen times before. It adds to the discussion and knowledge of lean; it does not imitate it. The concepts shared in this book are based on real application, not theory, and if applied, will accelerate and sustain your lean transformation.

As if writing a book was not difficult enough, picking a useful and original title has proven to be equally daunting. We are happy with the result, but given its unusual nature, an explanation is in order. *The Hitchhiker's Guide to Lean* reflects the authors' travels as well as the journeys upon which lean learners embark. By providing pragmatic and significant guideposts, we convey the lessons learned to help you strengthen your lean transformation.

Too many lean travelers get stuck in ruts, in which they remain, or end up abandoning their vehicles and returning to their old ways. They take the lessons learned from their first application, develop a model, and hang onto it, whether it is achieving results or not. The authors have experienced and witnessed many ruts and it is the speed at which you learn and change based on those lessons that counts in the long run. In this book you will read many stories of success and defeat, which we have experienced first-hand.

Successful lean programs incorporate past lessons, but also look forward for direction and progress. What would have happened if Toyota Production System greats Taiichi Ohno and Shigeo Shingo had solely looked back at what Henry Ford had accomplished? We all owe a debt to their forward thinking. The authors try to emulate the behaviors and attitudes of these masters by charting new territory and asking difficult questions. Like hitchhikers, lean practitioners sometimes do not know where the journey will lead, but the lessons of lean are incorporated each year, month, day, and moment. Imagine what it would be like if hitchhikers left each other a guide. This is what we have done, so you do not have to hit the road ignorant of the right path and the wrong turns.

In presenting the material in this book, the authors do not mean to imply they have reached some destination on the journey. Quite the contrary, the process of writing the book has taught us more and taken us down some roads that might have not otherwise been traveled. *The Hitchhiker's Guide to Lean* reflects what they consider to be the most critical lessons learned over their combined thirty-plus years of exploring the lean highways. The lean journey is never-ending. It will continue. And this book will help guide you as you hitchhike along your lean journey. We can not drop you off at the destination, but we can get you on the right road. If you follow it, you will achieve great gains.

The book's structure is unique. It does not focus on anything that has already been covered dozens of times in existing books. Readers will not see chapters devoted to work cells, value stream mapping, kaizen (a process of continuous improvement, often taking place in a team setting), Five S, or any other tools. Instead, *The Hitchhiker's Guide to Lean* shines a light on the areas where most lean efforts fail. Many companies attempt lean transformation, but far too few achieve success.

Whenever a speech is delivered by one of the authors, it has been a practice to poll the audience to find out who is familiar with lean. Nearly everyone has some knowledge, although it is generally specific to some tool set. Audience members are also asked whether their companies have begun lean transformations. The average hovers around 60%. They are then asked how many would consider their lean efforts to be outrageously successful . . . and the number drops to a small handful of companies. Any organization can achieve some performance gains by employing kaizen efforts, work cells, value stream mapping, or other tools. The authors' intent with this book is to help lean implementers move beyond the tools and take lean to a self-sustaining and continuously improving level. We want you to be among the audience members to raise your hand and say with confidence that your lean transformation is wildly successful. We want your program to accelerate with such momentum that it would be harder to stop than to keep going. By following the "hitchhiker" lessons, your organization will continue on into the stratosphere rather than plateau or fall back. This is why the authors consider this book to be a guide and not simply a how-to manual.

To make the lessons provided in this book simple for readers to remember, each topic is broken into five parts. Chapter One focuses on what is considered to be the most important lesson of all: Lean is not born from what you see, but from how you think. Five key principles are provided to guide lean behaviors from the top executives to the front-line personnel and throughout the company.

Chapter Two examines the five phases of the roadmap for lean transformation. There are no easy, standardized steps all organizations can follow to become lean—despite what some consultants and books profess. Each organization has its own unique set of business conditions and variables, including culture, issues, economics, resources, current state, and objectives. Each must craft its own unique lean journey. Unlike a simple recipe, the roadmap provides a lay of they land. You will not find a starting or end point (and all lean journeys truly have no end, they continue on a never-ending path towards improvement), but you will find a guide to help you develop your own journey.

The authors explore some common pitfalls of lean journeys in Chapter Three. These are the potholes that the roadmap might not warn against. Avoiding wrong turns is just as critical as following a lean journey's right path. This chapter provides advice to help you steer clear of the potholes.

In Chapter Four, the essential, and often misunderstood, topic of leadership is examined. Highlighted are five moves you can leverage as a leader to help drive your organization toward the ideal state. Leadership is about more than making a commitment and providing resources. It is more than providing a vision or being inspirational. Primarily, leadership is about creating change and moving an organization toward the ideal state. The skills today's leaders need to succeed are explored.

Chapter Five focuses on building an organization's operating system and its five dimensions: thinking, systems, tools, evaluation, and consistency. When used properly, an operating system can unite and expand an organization's improvement initiatives into an effective business model. It provides a litmus test to ensure every activity or decision remains consistent with where the organization is heading.

The first five chapters apply to lean at any stage of transformation and to any industry or function. The second section of the book explores more specific topics. Chapter Six, for example, focuses on the complex topic of lean accounting. It looks at how an organization can apply lean to accounting processes and activities and how accounting serves the rest of the organization. Material management, the subject of Chapter Seven, has typically focused on just-in-time. A fresh spin is given from a lean perspective. Chapter Eight highlights the different ways service organizations apply lean.

Most of the book focuses on organizational change, but Chapter Nine examines how individuals within an organization can apply lean. The authors frankly expect that this chapter will prove the most challenging for readers. It is about what you can do to improve yourself. We hope you are willing to join us for this leg of the journey.

The final section of the book includes interviews with five lean leaders. These champions are or have been on the frontlines of change at organizations of varying sizes and complexities. These leaders are the cast of characters the authors have met while hitchhiking along their journey.

Enough rambling. It's time to start hitchhiking. Stick out your thumb and hitch a ride on the lean journey. Remember, hitchhikers don't travel a fixed path. They intentionally wander so they can learn and change along the way. Eventually, you may want to pick up the next hitchhiker and offer your guidance. If you see someone looking for a lift, please slow down.

# Table of Contents

*The Hitchhiker's Guide to Lean: Lessons from the Road*

# 1

# Think First: Five Principles of Lean

The focus of any popular new concept is often on its application and results. But some fundamental assumptions and basic truths underlie the results. To become truly effective at anything, a person must understand these fundamentals. Without that understanding, an individual would just be mimicking others, which can lead to superficial gains and deceiving progress. But sustainable results require a first grasp of why and how the concepts are really applied. And so, this book begins with an exploration of the most fundamental truths underlying lean: five lean principles.

Look at the diet field as an example. Whatever the latest fad, the focus is on the weight loss, the recipes, and the practices. A scant few followers seek out the science or fundamental beliefs behind the diet. Those that do are better able to apply the practices, or modify them to fit their needs. The same tenets hold true when people try to dissect successful companies. Companies such as Wal-Mart, GE, and Dell have been benchmarked to no end and their practices copied verbatim. However, without understanding the fundamental truths that drive these powerhouses, the copycat companies never achieve comparable success. Lean has suffered the same fate.

Only a few companies achieve sustainable results by permanently and completely transforming themselves. Many companies practice lean, but they never truly internalize it as part of their basic code. Instead, most lean advocates explain the lean philosophy in one of two ways. First there is the lean religion approach, where gurus suggest executives take the lean transformation leap on faith. They claim practitioners can only understand lean after doing it, and any failure to take the leap is a failure of leadership. This approach has obvious flaws. The second camp makes an effort to explain lean beliefs, but they end up preaching about sacred cows—making it hard to separate the real meat from the fat. As a common example, it is agreed that "simplification" is a tenet of lean, but that is not what makes lean unique. Other promoters camouflage lean principles by packaging actions, practices, and tools as if they are philosophy or thinking.

Your lean transformation journey must begin with an understanding and acknowledgment of lean's true principles. It is the only way to drive behavior and set in motion the process for true change. Your beliefs will drive your behaviors; your behaviors will drive your actions; and your actions will generate results.

Imagine you are driving down the road. You have a working speedometer, gas pedal, and brake pedal. Your windshield is clear and you are alert. You see the speed limit sign. You know the law and the consequences for getting caught breaking it. But this does not control your behavior. Your beliefs and feelings about the speed limit, the law, safety, and other factors determine your behavior.

Many organizations try to change the behaviors of people by changing the tools or policies in the organization. This is generally very ineffective. Changing how people think is difficult work, so many companies try to take the easy way to affect behaviors using this less direct, however ineffective route. The first reason it is more difficult to change thinking and beliefs is that they are hard to see and measure. Also, beliefs are regarded as deeply personal. Leaders cannot force employees to change their beliefs. The only way to change behaviors, and ultimately the results of the organization, is to align employees with the company's belief systems.

Toyota Production System purists legitimately complain that any effort to boil lean down to a few key principles oversimplifies it and misses key points. But, to communicate any model, it must be simplified in some form. To be clear, it is not suggested that the following five principles comprise the comprehensive set of lean principles. They are, however, an effective group of principles. By clearly articulating what they are, their meaning, and the behaviors and tools that should be attached to each one, the reader is provided the right direction. Because lean transformation is a journey, the direction and speed at which you will be traveling will be more important than any single day's set of activities.

The five lean principles are:

1. Directly observe work as activities, connections, and flows;
2. Systematic waste elimination;
3. Establish high agreement of what and how;
4. Systematic problem solving; and
5. Create a learning organization.

Each principle carries its own meaning and set of behaviors. However, their essential value lies in how they work together. It is important to note that these principles have no sequential order. They are continually at work and guide how an organization's people react and respond to the events around them. Principles provide direction and surface when people are confronted with a crisis or challenge. It is easy to abide by principles when conditions are optimal. But what happens under pressure?

Consider Johnson & Johnson's principle that they would never knowingly harm a patient or customer. That sounds great. But how far would they go to honor that principle? Do you remember the Tylenol® scare? The actual problem was fairly limited in scope. Johnson & Johnson did not try to narrow down the potential risk to a few bottles, alert customers to identify the tainted bottles, or try to spin the message that it was not the company's fault. Instead, it immediately pulled the entire product line from the shelves. This was consistent with their principle. No matter what the cost, they were not going to risk harming a customer. Would your company give up its best-selling product and its revenues for something seemingly as insignificant as a principle?

As with Johnson & Johnson, principles should help companies make decisions. Many corporations spend time and money developing and distributing their values—essentially the same as principles. All major corporations at some time have included respect and integrity among these values. However, because they do not provide guidance for key decisions, principles such as these are not helpful. No one comes to work saying, "I was going to work without integrity today, but since it is a corporate value I will work with integrity."

## PRINCIPLE ONE: DIRECTLY OBSERVE WORK AS ACTIVITIES, CONNECTIONS, AND FLOWS

As shown in Figure 1-1, Principle One serves as the house's roof and provides shelter to the other four. For many organizations, the skills associated with this principle are among the most difficult to master of the five principles because of the subtleties involved. The majority of businesses not only contradict the principle, but are frequently in direct conflict with its practices.

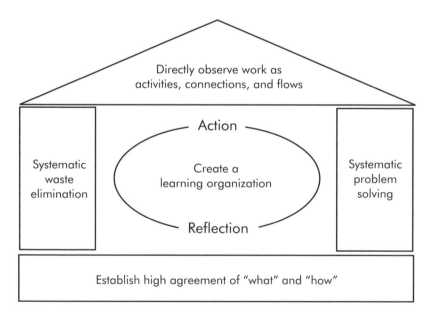

Figure 1-1. Shown is the house of lean principles and how it is built.

## Understanding Current Reality

Principle One describes *how* businesses understand their current reality and *what* criteria they are evaluating against when they ascertain their current reality. Most managers make decisions, solve problems, and take other action believing that they already understand the company's current reality. But they rarely take specific actions to increase their knowledge and understanding of the current reality. In addition, a common understanding of the current reality should be developed, not just an individual one. If this is done right, the rest becomes much easier. Most disagreements about the right solution, decision, or course of action are really disagreements about the interpretation of current reality.

Twelve years ago, the book *Reengineering the Corporation* popularized the reengineering movement. One of its central tenets (later revoked by one of the book's authors) was to throw away current reality (Hammer and Champy 1993). The original premise was that organizations should not be trapped by their current reality and should instead take out a clean sheet of paper to start over. The problem with this approach is that current reality contains a lot of valuable information. First, organizations probably already do some things well. Secondly, they have made and fixed many mistakes. If they throw away current reality, they are likely to throw away the good things they do today and repeat many of the mistakes made in the past. Lastly, how will they be able to gage whether they have improved if they do not have a sense of where they were at the beginning? How do you determine the measure of improvement?

Principle One is about how to understand current reality. Traditional practices for understanding current reality typically focus on results or outcomes. Almost all data is about what a process produces. Most stories and reports also focus on outcomes. This principle focuses on current reality at its source. It is about understanding the means—not just the ends.

Principle One is a difficult principle in terms of the skill and practice that it requires. It is not more important than the other principles, but it is difficult to adopt because it typically defies conventional wisdom. Once an organization gets in sync with Principle One, the other four principles will be adopted more easily.

## Directly Observing Work

Directly observing work often involves a sophisticated but readily available tool: the eyes. In lean, "going to the gemba" is often talked about. The phrase means going to the shop floor or where work is actually performed. But, there is a lot more to it than that. You may remember all the hoopla about management by walking around (MBWA). It was a great concept with one major flaw: walking around looked more like a stroll through the park or industrial tourism than a structured process to understand current reality. It is one thing to be out in the operation or where work is occurring. It is something altogether different to use a structured method to observe, analyze, and understand how work is done and why it is done that way. Try this exercise as a test: pick a process that you have walked past many times and think you know well. Pick a spot—literally a spot to stand—and watch the process for one hour. Do nothing but observe current reality to help you understand how and why the process is working. It is guaranteed that you will see things you have never seen before.

To use an analogy about Principle One, assume there are several bird feeders and some trees that are great for birds outside your kitchen window. You enjoy watching the birds gather for breakfast. However, thanks to a neighborhood hawk, they occasionally become breakfast. So it can be said that you watch birds. However, you are by no means a bird-watcher. There is a huge difference. A bird-watcher has tools, a process, and a framework for interpreting observations. Although you and the bird-watcher may see the same thing, a bird-watcher would observe much more detail than you. Similarly, many people observe processes, but few are actual process observers.

Directly observing work involves more than "going to the gemba." It encompasses many different behaviors. Quality of information is emphasized over quantity of information. There is a big push in businesses today to gather and make available more and more information, including real-time information. But that does not make it quality information. The person who believes in directly observing work seeks a single quality piece of information, the needle in the haystack, which would really help him or her take the right action. This principle seeks to build a common view versus arguing over the "right" view. Many meetings to discuss current reality devolve into arguments about what is "really" wrong with the process and what is "really" happening. Everyone has his or her own view. Participants try to figure out who has the right view; if they cannot decide, those with power or authority make the final determination.

If you stood facing someone and drew a circle in the air, in which way would the circle be formed? For one of you, it would be clockwise, the other, counter-clockwise. Which is right? Both answers are right, but they are also incomplete. Most statements about current reality are not wrong; they are incomplete. The person who adopts this principle seeks to put multiple views of current reality together to build one common and more complete view of it. Tools such as value stream mapping, process mapping, videotaping, and flow diagrams (sometimes called spaghetti diagrams) are designed for exactly this purpose. They help connect everyone's views and focus attention on the process and the means instead of just the results or ends.

### Activities, Connections, and Flows

The second part of Principle One concerns the frameworks companies or individuals use when they observe. Most people see things such as equipment, people, material, and information. These are parts of the process, but they are not the process itself. The process is made up of three elements: activities, connections, and flows as shown in Figure 1-2. Consider these the building blocks or the neutrons, protons, and electrons of the process world. Any one of them may involve multiple people and tools. The ability to observe in this way leads to a

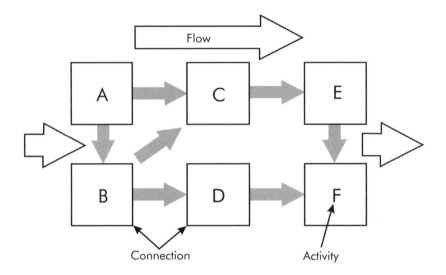

*Figure 1-2. Activities, connections, and flows are the building blocks of any process.*

more structured way to make improvements. The genesis of this framework is important. Two Harvard professors, H. Kent Bowen and Steven Spear, spent time in Toyota's factories interpreting how the company really accomplished, designed, managed, and improved work. This was not a passive activity; they actually participated in performing the work (Bowen and Spear 1999; Spear 1999). The framework of activities, connections, and flows describes how people at Toyota see the process as they observe it.

*Activities* are the steps taken, such as machining a part, solving a problem, making a decision, or taking an order, to produce a result. The point of the framework is that people do not produce results all by themselves any more than machines do; activities produce results. If people cannot interpret the entire activity, they might fix, improve, or change the wrong element of the activity. Ask yourself the following questions about activities at your organization:

- What is the expected result of the activity?
- Will the result be clearly understood?
- How is the activity structured?
- Is the sequence determined?
- Is the method specific?
- Is the timing specific?
- How will the organization know whether it meets the expected outcome?

*Connections* are how the customer/supplier pairs functions together. Every business relationship has a customer/supplier connection: someone wants something (customer), be it material, information, help, or even a raise, which someone else must provide (supplier). The internal customer/supplier relationships are different than those with a company's external customers. They are not based on concepts such as, "The customer is always right." In these cases, the customer merely needs something and has as much responsibility for an effective customer/supplier relationship as does the supplier. There should be only one way to make a request and one way to respond. Organizations should be able to know when the customer/supplier relationship breaks down.

When most people visit a company with a Toyota-like andon system, they see the overhead cord, hear the music that goes off to indicate when someone pulls the cord, note the operator's position, and observe the lights that indicate status and location. When most organizations copy such a system, they try to duplicate what they have seen based on a limited understanding of the current reality. What actually exists is a customer/supplier connection whereby an operator is a customer, and the supervisor is a supplier of help or assistance. Pulling the andon cord is the only way to make a request (even when the supervisor is an arm's length away). When it fails (if, for example, the supervisor fails to show up), the entire line stops, indicating to the manager there is a problem. If managers do not understand the underlying customer/supplier relationship, they could hang all the andon cords they want, but the system would be doomed to failure.

The last element of Principle One is flow. *Flows* are the paths, or routes, that material, information, and people take. The focal point is typically material and its flow through the operation. Companies often pay more attention to activities than flow, because they are generally more involved in performing activities. However, flows cut across the white space in processes. They should be simple, meaning that they do not cause too much waste; and specific, meaning there is one path through the process. Problem indicators include forks and loops in the flow path.

Consider a requisition as an example. Most requisitions require a few minutes of actual work time. But lead time can takes weeks or months. Why is there such a disconnect? Because most companies design their requisition process to be convenient for the people approving them, they ignore the perspective of the requisition itself. What happens when someone "walks it through," a common workaround for a bad process? A requisition is completed in hours, instead of days. The people walking it through have the perspective of the requisition itself and cannot abide the waste of the normal turnaround.

A common lean tool, the U-shaped cell, is another example. Although it has been around for decades, it is still often misapplied. Both simple and specific, the U-shaped cell is a great example of proper flow. However, it is not advisable to build airplanes or design a hospital operating room using U-shaped cells (an arrangement of equipment into a smooth process in the shape of a "U"). Doing so could make the processes worse. The authors know of one company that required, to the point of absurdity, U-shaped cells throughout all of its plants. A complicated part traveled from one U-shaped cell to another, fulfilling the mandate but violating the objective of simple and specific flow.

## PRINCIPLE TWO: SYSTEMATIC WASTE ELIMINATION

Systematic waste elimination is the granddaddy of lean principles. Although it is a gross mis-statement and misleading to companies trying to make lean work, lean is typically characterized as nothing more than the elimination of waste. The misrepresentation persists in part because books, magazines, speakers, and practitioners perpetuate the myth. Also, the elimination of waste is more tangible, simpler, direct, and easier to measure than the other principles.

Lean trainers often depict waste as the sole justification for lean—the end for all of lean's other means. However, waste, or more specifically the elimination of waste, is both a lean tool and principle. Those engaged in lean transformation actively pursue and think about eliminating waste every day.

If you believe you are part of a lean organization, ask these questions:

- How many people use the language of waste every day?
- Does every employee have at least one specific mechanism to engage directly in the elimination of waste?
- When talking about problems or opportunities, do you apply the lens of waste every time?
- How much time do people, particularly leaders, spend specifically looking throughout the organization for waste?

Most employees of companies that win accolades for their lean efforts cannot answer these questions in ways that indicate they truly grasp Principle Two.

Waste elimination is certainly not a new lean transformation topic. But it needs to be looked at it in new ways. Waste is not just a reason for lean. Lean takes a wider scope, addressing, among other things, the relentless pursuit and elimination of waste through a common lens and language.

## The Language of Waste

Principle Two requires a lens and a language specific to the relentless pursuit and elimination of waste. Basically, *waste* is defined as anything beyond the absolute minimum amount of materials, manpower, and machinery needed to add value to a product or service.

There are seven types of waste:

1. Overproduction—Producing more than the immediate customer needs or producing something sooner than it is needed.

2. Transportation—Any movement of material, paper, or information including shipping, moving, carrying, or even lifting.

3. Inventory—Stockpiled parts, orders, time, or activities. Inventory protects companies from other forms of waste, and makes them less willing to work on other forms of waste. Unless companies add value to inventory, it is waste. It can cost companies in many ways, but put simply, inventory is money sleeping.

4. Motion—Any movement by people, including walking, bending, and reaching, which is not directly related to value-added work.

5. Waiting—Any downtime products or people spend waiting for material, information, or people.

6. Overprocessing—Doing more to a product or process than the customer requires. This includes over-automation, over-computerization, and over-mechanization.

7. Defects—Any process, product, or service error. The worst kinds of defects are those that reach the customer; but defects that companies correct within the process use tremendous resources and are often hidden and unresolved.

Many companies view number seven as the waste of correction instead of the waste of defects. The reason seems to be a case of not actively using the seven wastes as a lens every single day. A company should not stop correcting defects; but it should seek out the defect at its source and eliminate the waste of creating the defect in the first place. If a company's people are currently in the waste of correction mindset, what is to be done when correction is already found in the process but defects persist?

Before discussing other wastes, it should be made clear why having a language for waste is so important. The seven wastes are not to be used as an academic exercise to see how organizations can categorize things. They comprise a specific lens companies should use every day. The Eskimos have dozens of different words to describe snow, and each one has a slightly different meaning. Beyond their language value, the words for snow provide the Eskimos with a lens. They can use the words to distinguish dozens of types of snow. How many different types of snow can you distinguish? By having a specific language, companies use a common lens that enables them to see waste. By deeply embedding the seven wastes "language," organizations see opportunities that were not previously apparent. By using a common language, their eyes are more open.

Taiichi Ohno, a founding father of the Toyota Production System, originally developed the concept of the seven wastes. Many people have tried to improve on the original, but they generally fall short. A commonly added eighth waste is that of underutilized people. This is not a reference to people who are not loaded with enough work; it is not using the full potential of the individual, specifically the brain, to add value to the organization. In general, lean will address this, giving people the lens, language, and mechanisms to engage all employees. However, included as one of the wastes, it does not serve a purpose. The seven wastes are a lens for observing and eliminating waste. You can walk into a process and see an operator who has to walk too far to retrieve parts from a parts bin, or watch a requisition form wait, or watch a machine produce a defect, but you can not observe and eliminate on the spot the fact that a person is not utilized to his or her full potential. While significant, underutilized people do not warrant equal billing with the seven wastes.

Other added wastes, many of which fall outside of manufacturing, are usually nothing more than variations of the original seven. For example, the waste of too many people in a meeting is really the waste of overprocessing—using more resources (for example, ten people) than necessary (three people) to add value (make a decision); waste of information may be categorized as the waste of overproduction (producing more information than necessary), overprocessing (doing more to the information than necessary), or inventory (storing more information than necessary).

As a tool, the original seven wastes work quite well to help organizations identify and eliminate waste. Organizations need to take the concepts beyond the classroom, however, and make them part of every meeting and improvement effort. As an example, a home healthcare organization began to explicitly use the lens and language of the seven wastes. It was common practice for its visiting nurses to complete a referral file and prepare the proper materials for each site or home they were to visit each day. They had been preparing their materials in advance. When a visit was cancelled, they had excess materials or excess work in returning the materials. A long lead time to refer patients and request services had been causing the overproduction. The agency dramatically reduced the cycle time and significantly reduced overproduction. The home healthcare organization never recognized its wasteful practices until it adopted the lens and language for identifying and eliminating waste.

## Value Added

The last element of Principle Two is value added, a key element in determining waste. Many people confuse the value-added/non-value-added distinction with the definition of waste. While they are closely related concepts, they are not the same. Something can be value added (drilling a hole) but still wasteful (drilling it deeper or to a greater precision than is necessary). The two lenses are both unique and useful. For an activity to be value added it must meet three criteria:

1. The customer must value it and be willing to pay for it.
2. It must change the form, fit, or function of the product or service.
3. It must be done right the first time.

To be value-added, an activity must meet all three criteria for the following reasons: first, the three criteria provide the organization with a common understanding of value added; and second, it prevents organizations from missing opportunities by inadvertently classifying an activity as value added. Once someone identifies something as value added, the organization accepts and agrees that it must remain. The rigorous definition is quite effective for exposing potential in the organization.

In most processes, value added represents less than 1% of the timeline. To increase its percentage, organizations can either add more value or eliminate non-value-added activities. Most efforts focus on eliminating non-value-added activities, since they are easier to identify and fix.

It is important to understand that the second an organization calls something "value added," it becomes untouchable. It can, however, continue to explore the activity. As an example, using the lens of value added, an automotive dealership discussed whether or not its waiting room was value added. The argument was that because customers prefer a clean waiting room with coffee and TV, and not having one would pose many problems, the waiting room must be value added. It was not suggested that the dealership should eliminate its waiting room, but looking at it as non-value added raised important questions. For example, customers waited 45–60 minutes in the waiting room for an oil change. What could the dealership do differently if it had no waiting room? The drive-through quick oil change franchises provided a model. They have a team, a process, and the customer never has to wait more than 15 minutes (although the oil change still has to be done right the first time). By challenging the waiting room as being non-value added, the dealership may not have eliminated it, but new ways were found to reduce the amount of time customers had to wait there.

How about adding value? This is often a forgotten edge of the value-added/non-value-added sword. Consider the cell phone industry. Some improvements focus on removing waste: make it smaller, cheaper, and less likely to drop calls. But most improvements are based on adding value: email, pictures, photos, games, and more. Look at both ends of the spectrum to maximize opportunities.

## PRINCIPLE THREE: ESTABLISH HIGH AGREEMENT OF WHAT AND HOW

In a word, Principle Three is the lean concept of standardization. However, it goes beyond standardized work and Five S, a method of structuring the work environment to spot problems quickly and eliminate waste. "Establish high agreement of what and how" is the foundation principle, because everything else builds upon it. The phrase "standardization" may imply "high agreement"; however, there is a significant difference in connotation. Standardization often implies, although typically not intended, that a standard be applied to someone: *This* is how you will do your activity. "High agreement" means that the people closest to an activity or process should be in agreement about what and how an activity or process should be accomplished.

Another definition for the high agreement principle is, "Valuing a common way or process with low ambiguity more than you value your own way." To be clear, this definition does not mean that individuals need to like the common way, but they value having the agreement and accept decisions that they may not like. The definition speaks to the importance of having principles. Imagine there is a problem with safety regarding the mixing of fork truck and people traffic. As a solution, new walkways, in which all people are supposed to walk, are devised. An employee could decide that he or she knows how to be safe in a factory, and the walkways are unnecessary. But applying the principle means that the employee will nonetheless use the walkways because he or she values the common way. Most people are able to see the principle's benefits, but find it hard to accept because it means giving up their own ways.

To explore why Principle Three is so important, the focus is turned on its second half: "what and how." Organizations spend most of their time on the "what," but overlook the "how." The "whats" are the goals, objectives, tasks, and measures to which all agree. "How" refers to the specific processes, methods, and rules organizations use to achieve the "whats," or the goals.

In an earlier principle, the andon system was briefly explained. Here is how this principle applies to the andon system. The "what" in this case has two parts. First, the objective is zero defects. Companies may never get there, but that is the goal. The second part invokes a rule: do not pass on defects to the next activity. This is much more specific, but there may be many "hows" to achieve that "what." To review, if participants in an andon system see a problem, they pull the andon cord that triggers a light and music. Team leaders show up to review the problem and render decisions. Imagine if you were a team member and every team leader had his own "how" to achieve that goal; one might use the andon cord; another asks you to yell when you need help; a third leader wants you to submit the problems in writing; and a fourth leader tries to find and fix the problems. As a team member, you would be living in chaos. And your team would essentially have no system to maintain or improve to achieve your goals. Without spending time on a specific "how," the "what" part of high agreement is doomed.

For another example, consider the U.S. road system. Each day, 100 million Americans drive at high speeds in heavy pieces of equipment over varying road conditions. They survive with amazingly little incident. It may not seem like it, but the roadways are quite successful given the sheer magnitude of opportunity for failure. It is fair to say that drivers have high agreement about the goal: get to the destination as quickly and safely as possible. Now imagine if drivers agreed on the "what," but had different "hows" to achieve it. Some might drive on the left side of the road; others might go at red lights. It would be chaos. There is not chaos because everyone agrees on the "hows": drive on the right side of the road, red means stop, and do not cross the double-yellow lines, for example. In reality, 100 million drivers never sat in a 12-hour planning meeting together, nor do they report to the same boss; but they are able to navigate the nation's highways with less chaos than most 50-person departments.

The next time you attend a meeting, note how much of the conversation focuses on the "what" versus the "how." Do not allow yourself to get tricked. Statements such as "buckle down on suppliers," or "solve the customer problem," or "cut spending" sound like "hows," but are really objectives; they can be achieved through many different means. By failing to focus on the "how," many people walk away from meetings filled with ambiguity and thus are prone to disconnects.

Establishing high agreement takes more than tools, but many lean tools are specifically designed to enable agreement, including Five S, standardized work, visual controls, error proofing, master scheduling, control point standardization, and hoshin planning. Remember Principle Three's definition: "valuing a common way or process with low ambiguity more than you value your own way." If people are not engaged to believe in this principle, it is likely they will undervalue the tools and ultimately undermine them.

## PRINCIPLE FOUR: SYSTEMATIC PROBLEM SOLVING

Principle Four, systematic problem solving, is not about whether organizations solve problems (everybody does), but how they think about and look at problems. In general, problems are viewed as a negative thing. Some companies go so far as to avoid use of the word "problem." Obviously, avoiding use of the word does not actually result in fewer problems. In a lean organization, problems are opportunities. True, by calling them "opportunities," they sound less intimidating—but lean organizations actually view problems as opportunities.

Companies should value finding and resolving small problems as well as large ones. It is not that small problems are as significant as larger ones. A part being late, the equipment being down, or a person not following standard work instructions do not seem as valuable to work on as a defect that affects a customer or a budget shortfall. However, the overall impact of thousands of ignored small problems outweighs the impact of just a handful of large problems. Also, when a problem first occurs, organizations do not know in advance whether the problem will deliver a major or minor impact. A lean organization does not wait to see how far the problem will go. The problem is solved before it has a chance to get out of hand.

Systematic problem solving is not about whether problems are solved, nor is it about the tools used. It is about how organizations view problems, expose them, and deal with them. Regardless of the tools and skill sets, if a company gets this principle right, it will gain greater leverage from problems. Since companies have to deal with problems anyway, they may as well get more mileage for the effort.

## Probing Deeper

Problems can reveal important things. In most organizations, a problem is simply an adverse condition that must be resolved: the equipment failed, the customer left, or the supplier missed a shipment, for example. When the conditions present themselves, companies get the equipment running, campaign to woo the customer back, and pressure the supplier to improve. Lean organizations address the solution but go a step further by asking what the condition tells them about their systems and processes. For example, they might ponder:

- Why didn't our maintenance processes catch the problem before the equipment failed?
- In what ways are we failing our customers?
- Who is the next potential customer to leave us?
- Why is our supplier development process not identifying problems before we miss shipments?

These are deeper questions. Answering them will help make the processes stronger.

Compare how you solve problems at work with family problems at home. You probably approach them differently. If an employee comes to you and says he identified a product defect, you will probably focus on fixing the defect as quickly and effectively as possible. If your child brings home a bad report card, however, what is your concern? Is it the report card? Or is it your child and what might be going on that will affect his future plans? The lean perspective applies a concern for the future to all problems: what does this problem tell me about my ability to be successful in the future? When you encounter the next few problems, delve deeper and you will broaden your perspective.

What happens next? A broader perspective leads to several different behaviors:

1. Organizations stay with problems longer and dig deeper.

2. Problems are immediately brought to the surface.

3. Work is designed to reveal when problems exist.

4. Small problems are valued as highly as large ones.

## Five Whys

Despite conventional wisdom, organizations should *not* dispatch problems as quickly as possible. They should contain them as quickly as possible and remove the symptoms, staying with the problem until they are sure they have the right answer. This often means going past the obvious cause and peeling back a few more layers until the core problem is revealed. The five whys is a tool designed for this purpose. By asking "why?" five times, inquisitors can get to the root cause of a problem. There is nothing magical about the number five; sometimes it takes two, other times nine. The root cause is related to whether problems can be ascribed to activities, connections, or flows (see Principle One). Using five whys is not particularly complicated. It is frequently written about and taught. Yet, few companies on the lean journey apply it regularly. Using the five whys requires three things:

1. A commitment to the underlying principle that drives the desire to dig deeper.

2. The discipline and stamina to stay with the problem.

3. Validation of each "why" answer by checking if it would remove the previous answer.

The reason the second and third factors are so important is that while some problems can be solved in the hallway, many "why" answers take extensive investigation and exploration (often requiring the direct observation of work). It might take days, weeks, or months to tackle all five whys if the answers are not immediately evident. If this principle is not embedded in the organization, people will likely move on before getting to the root cause of problems.

As a simple example, consider a piece of equipment that fails at a plant. The leader asks, "Why did the equipment fail?" The technician answers, "Because the circuit board burned out."

Typically, the next question is, "How long until you can have it running again?" But, the lean leader also asks, "Why did the circuit board burn out?" The technician responds, "Because it overheated." This leads to, "Why did it overheat?" And, the response is, "Because it is not getting enough air."

If the technician and the lean leader stopped there, they could have permanently removed the symptom, but they would not have drilled down to the larger problem. They could have opened the control panel door and pointed a fan at it. Many factories use similar temporary solutions—in most cases for the long term. But the lean leader continued with his queries. "Why is the circuit board not getting enough air?" The response, "Because the filter is clogged," was countered with, "Why wasn't the filter changed?" When a "why?" is met with silence it is a good indicator that the exercise is getting close to the root cause. In this case, after some discussion, the reply was, "Because there is no preventive maintenance schedule." Can you guess what they developed after the exercise? This example illustrates the connections—the customer was the equipment and the schedule, request, and technician were the suppliers.

There is nothing magical about the five whys. Just about any problem-solving tool will work as well, but organizations must ascribe to the underlying principle.

The second behavior related to Principle Four is to immediately bring problems to the surface. Because problems are generally considered negative, most organizations tend to ignore them until they exhaust every other possibility. Here is a key question: Does the problem exist whether or not the organization exposes it? The answer, of course, is yes. Companies know the problems are out there, so they should celebrate when they are uncovered. Similarly, even though they may be suffering with an ailment, many people do not want to visit a doctor, because they are afraid that the doctor might diagnose the problem.

In returning to the andon system example, the process has one purpose: to expose problems immediately. The rule is that any problem, no matter how large or small, triggers the system. If a work process is off by two seconds, a team could try to speed up and raise the red flag only if they are unable catch up. According to the rule, however, employees pull the andon cord as soon as they fall two seconds behind. The team leader tries to assess the situation and develop a remedy. Even if the team member solves the problem before the team leader arrives, it is still important to assess the problem. A good team leader will delve deeper and ask, "What in our process led to us to falling behind? How can we make it easier to stay on track?"

To immediately bring problems to the surface, organizations have to design their work to expose problems as they occur. Using commuting to work as an example, drivers may know how long the overall trip will take them, but they also know where they should be five minutes into their drive, at the 10-minute mark, and at other points along the route. They know they are behind before they pull into the company's parking lot, because they had indicators along the way. Similarly, in a lean system, work and processes tell organizations about problems before it is too late.

Kanban and just-in-time are great examples. For decades, just-in-time has been positioned as an inventory management and reduction tool. But its primary purpose is to create a visual system that exposes problems as they occur. If a company has a pull between two process steps and its inventory climbs and blocks the upstream process, it is known right away, not when the nightly or monthly reports come in or when someone calls out the problem on the plant radio. If a company has two unstable processes, it may be able to operate normally with five kanbans. Under extreme conditions, however, it may require 10 kanbans of the same size to keep operating. A company with a misguided sense of lean might be inclined to run with five kanbans anyway, but the plant would quickly grind to a halt. It would also be incorrect for an organization to continue running with 10 kanbans under the misguided notion that it would therefore be protected from unstable process slowdowns. Yes, it would need the protection, but more importantly, it would need the learning. If a company believes that exposing problems is important, it would set up a pull system with five kanbans, and then put another five off to the side under lock and key. When the company dips into the security stock, it should also be undertaking some deep problem solving. The company would be using pull as a method to expose problems as they occur, as well as to control inventory.

Cycle-timing marks, the marks on the floor or on a conveyor (for an assembly process) that indicate equal increments of time being consumed, offer another example. Assuming a process takes 100 seconds, there might be 10 marks, each indicating 10 seconds. These are used in part to help an operator keep pace. But more importantly, they quickly expose problems. If an operator knows where he is supposed to be when he passes over the sixth line, and he is not at that point, he immediately knows he has a problem. He can intervene before the process ends up "in the hole."

## PRINCIPLE FIVE: CREATE A LEARNING ORGANIZATION

The reason it is difficult to pin down a concrete, static definition of lean is that the very nature of lean is to change and improve—based on learning. The fifth lean principle, creating a learning organization, is referred to as the *glue* principle because it holds the other four principles together. Principle Five is the driving force that enables the others to be more than one-shot improvement efforts.

Much has been written about learning organizations; however, it is mostly born in academia and not practice. A true lean learning organization is pragmatic and learns from its improvement efforts. A lean learning organization uses its processes as laboratories and its employees as scientists.

Many companies have gone through significant lean transformations. They have improved their process layouts, established standardized work and visual management, built pull systems from their customers to their suppliers, and leveled work. Most of these companies have reached a plateau. The percentages by which they improve drop significantly over time, and while they continue to improve, their lean journey is largely considered over. These companies may have successfully incorporated lean's first four principles, but they have failed to integrate learning. In comparison, Toyota continues to make significant gains after more than 50 years on its lean journey. The difference is that every improvement, every solved problem, and every new idea at Toyota generates more learning, more capability, and more skill. This is what a learning organization is really about. Very few companies continue to pound away on lean every year; but it is the hallmark of a truly lean organization.

## Experimentation

Experimentation and reflection are the driving forces of lean learning. They are also core to practical learning, which distinguishes information from ability, and knowledge from know-how. Most learning in organizations is focused on the gathering, dissemination, and validation of information. Information is important, but by itself it does not produce results. Most education is focused on gathering information and knowledge. But know-how and capability are different in that they measure results. The mantra here is that it is more important to be effective than right. To highlight the distinction, you may know the "right" way to develop a process. But, if you cannot gain people's confidence, impart understanding, or make changes happen, then you lack know-how. It does not matter if it is a people, organizational, or a technical barrier. Know-how and practical learning focus on breaking through barriers. The customer, shareholder, or employee does not really care what you know; they care about what you can do. A truly lean company is focused on what it can accomplish.

## Plan-do-check-act

Experimentation is the primary mechanism through which practical learning is generated. *Experimentation* means, at its most fundamental level, that organizations test each improvement or solution to verify that it achieves the anticipated results. This is, in essence, the familiar plan-do-check-act cycle.

Around for well over half a century, lean organizations rarely apply this fundamental concept. They might do a little planning, place emphasis on the "do," and largely ignore the "check" process. They most often "act" by starting over with a new plan.

Experimentation means that the plan must include a hypothesis. A *hypothesis* is a problem statement, a planned change and, most importantly, the expected result that this change will cause. To develop a hypothesis, an organization must first deeply understand the current reality of its process. Given how poorly most companies understand their current reality, it is easy to see why they do not typically start improvements with a hypothesis.

The "do" process in a practical learning environment is unique. Instead of merely implementing the solution, an organization first tests the idea, based on a hypothesis, as quickly and cheaply as possible. Generally, if an operator said it would be better for his process if he had a small table next to his machine, his organization would assign an engineer to design the table and a millwright to build it. Once it was built, they would see whether it actually works. Even if it did not really work, they might leave it because of all the time and money they sank into it. To conduct an experiment, however, someone might test the process by grabbing a small piece of plywood and using it as a table for 30 minutes. That way, the organization could determine whether the table works before assigning resources to the project.

The "check" part of the process is the most essential step. It is more important to learn about a process than to verify that the solution actually works. Lean leaders are students of their processes. When they oversee a process that yields an unexpected 3% differential in improvement, they do not just celebrate their success. They go back to discover why they did not anticipate the 3% gain.

"Act" is the final step of the loop. If they get the results they expect, organizations standardize the new solution. If they got different results, they go back to their plans to figure out why and strategize the next step. It is important to note that the learning generated during these steps does not end with "act." Done correctly, this generates the next plan. One improvement therefore turns into 10 improvements, 10 turns into 100, and 100 turns into 1,000 as the cycle perpetuates.

## Reflection

The second part of creating a learning environment involves reflection, which is more subjective than experimentation. Even so, organizations should still base reflection on real activities and results. Often, however, the issues are less measurable and testable than during experiments.

A great example of a reflection tool is the After Action Review. Created by the U.S. Army, it is a structured process to generate learning based on the real results of a mission or training exercise. The learning is immediately applied to the next event. It is a simple tool that can be applied to anything from improving staff meetings to launching new products. The After Action Review incorporates four questions that are generally presented as:

1. What was supposed to happen?
2. What did happen and why (deep understanding of current reality)?
3. What can we learn from our success and failure?
4. What will we do differently?

It is important to note that the process is not based on theory, anticipation, or guessing, but on real experiences. The four questions are meaningless outside of a true learning organization—there would be only four questions with no learning.

In 1999, there was a small but telling event at Toyota. The *Harvard Business Review* praised the company as being one of the world's best manufacturers (Spear and Bowen 1999). Instead of celebrations and press releases, Toyota's president Fujio Cho wrote a letter to the publication. The last line of his letter is most telling: "[This article] has helped us focus on reflection on how we can get closer to True North." Cho and the

Toyota organization used the article as a learning experience. They actively reflected on it and put the lessons they learned into action.

## Comfort and Fear

An organization that attempts to adopt learning, experimentation, and reflection sometimes faces some formidable barriers, including comfort and fear zones. The comfort zone encompasses the things an organization already knows how to do. Although it is where an organization is most at ease, learning cannot take place if it never steps outside of its comfort zone. But if a company steps too far, it treads into its fear zone. In the fear zone, a company's people fear for their physical, emotional, and/or professional safety. People cannot learn in the fear zone either. Therefore, most organizations have very narrow learning zones. How can they expand them?

First, organizations must acknowledge that they cannot eliminate fear. Companies that allow anyone to experiment with anything at anytime are in chaos. But they can establish order by ensuring the professional and emotional safety of those willing to break out and try new things. They can also clearly establish boundaries. If a company's people do not know the line beyond which they should not cross, they are likely to imagine it is closer than its actual location. Therefore, by clearly demarcating the fences, an organization can actually expand its opportunities.

Another way an organization can expand its learning zone is by shrinking its comfort zone. A truly lean organization forbids its people to do what they did yesterday. Learning and experimentation are expected and required for every job.

## Time

A significant barrier to learning is time. Most people and companies feel that they do not have the time to experiment and reflect. It is less an indication of available time, however, and more a signal that organizations do not *value* learning and reflection. Most people do not consider it real work. This forces people to do most of their reflection on their commutes home where their thoughts vanish into thin air. Leaders must make learning and reflection priorities. The single biggest failure of leadership is a failure to reflect. Leaders fail to stop and ask the questions that can lead to tomorrow's improvements, such as:

- Are our principles serving us well?
- Do we have the right skills?
- Is our toolbox effective?
- What is our customer expecting and how are we doing against that expectation?
- What assumptions about our business are no longer valid?

Leaders may ask these questions, but do they commit serious time to reflect on them? And most importantly, do they apply the results? Actions indeed speak louder than words when it comes to applying the principle of creating a learning organization.

## REFERENCES

Hammer, Michael and Champy, James. 1993. *Reengineering the Corporation: A Manifesto for Business Revolution*. New York: Harper Business.

Spear, Steven and Bowen, H. Kent. 1999. "Decoding the DNA of the Toyota Production System." *Harvard Business Review,* September 1.

Spear, Steven. 1999. *The Toyota Production System: An Example of Managing Complex Social/Technical Systems*. "5 Rules for Designing, Operating, and Improving Activities, Activity Connections, and Flow Paths." Dissertation, May 26, Harvard University Graduate School of Business Administration.

**Five Principles of Lean**

1. Directly observe work as activities, connections, and flows

2. Systematic waste elimination

3. Establish high agreement of what and how

4. Systematic problem solving

5. Create a learning organization

**2**

# People Need Leadership, Not Management: Five Leadership Moves for Lean

Why is leadership such an important topic in lean transformation? Because lean is not something you can engineer, implement through policy, or manage like a product launch. Lean changes everything when done right. It changes the way you think, talk, see, act, and react. It is a battle for people's minds and hearts, and such battles require leadership.

"Leadership" has become such a cliché, it has nearly lost all meaning. The word has almost become synonymous with "executive" and "management." Companies have built it into job titles—even ultra-lean Toyota. However, leadership is not a title or job; it is an *act*. *Leadership* is an act that anyone can conduct at any level in an organization. Including the word "leadership" in a job title or being known as an executive does not give a person the exclusive right to perform leadership acts (sometimes it may even make it more difficult to conduct acts of leadership).

To help define leadership, it is helpful to distinguish it from management. Managers maintain the status quo, or current reality. An organization's current reality does not plod along on its own. It takes a significant amount of effort and attention—from management—to keep the cogs spinning in place. Leadership, in contrast, moves a company and its component parts toward the ideal state. Any behavior that moves an organization one step closer to its never-achievable ideal state is an act of leadership. This is true regardless of an individual's position, regardless of whether anyone notices the act, and regardless of how the act fits into any leadership framework.

Many classic traits, such as motivation, communication, coaching, vision, and calmness, often characterize leadership. But traits alone do not constitute leadership. If actions do not move things forward toward the ideal state, there is no leadership. By its very definition, leadership requires leading people somewhere. Leaders cannot lead people if people remain fixed in place.

There are five leadership moves—five essential actions a leader can perform to help provide leadership on the lean journey.

## LEADERSHIP MOVE ONE: LEADERS MUST BE TEACHERS

"Teaching" does not necessarily mean standing in front of a classroom and delivering a lecture. Teachers need to be able to transfer ideas, skill, and understanding to others. Teaching might involve many tasks, but it is best exemplified when a student can declare that he or she is more capable today because of what a teacher did yesterday. In a lean organization, learning is critical. It is not a task for human resources to perform with skills assessments and in-company universities. It is line management's direct responsibility. Skills and knowledge are too important to ignore on a daily basis. Rather than focusing exclusively on the crises of the day, managers should take time to teach and provide leadership.

Why not delegate teaching to an external or internal training department? Because lean is based on how people think, not on just a set of tools or skills. Simply defined, *lean* is shared thinking. Those in the organization must share a common philosophy, a common set of ideas, and a common set of principles. This does not imply brainwashing or call for the elimination of diversity. It does speak, however, to how companies *apply* diversity. If everyone applies decisions and solutions based on different sets of ideas, the solutions often work against each other.

Individually, the solutions may all be "right," but collectively they can become counterproductive and destructive. Leaders cannot merely put people into situations and hope they learn the right things. Leaders must take responsibility for the message and for what is being learned. This is best accomplished when students can combine real-life experience with direct coaching from leaders.

An organization's principles should become guideposts and help people make tough decisions. When Enron collapsed, people often talked about its corporate values, or principles: integrity, respect, business excellence, and communication. Studies indicate that in past years almost half of large corporations in the U.S. include respect and integrity among their corporate values. These are not useful or effective principles—not because they are not followed, but because they do not help people make tough decisions. No one goes to work thinking, "I was going to forget about integrity today, but since I see that it is a corporate principle, I will act with integrity."

## LEADERSHIP MOVE TWO: BUILD TENSION, NOT STRESS

A lean leader must provide the source of energy that will compel the organization toward action. Without this energy, no amount of skill or knowledge will lead to success. Many leaders push their organizations but do not generate a corresponding sense of urgency. They create stress, but not tension. To distinguish the two, people feel stress when conditions are nearly impossible, pressures are immense, and the path forward is shrouded in fog. On the other hand, people experience tension when they sense a gap between the current reality and the ideal state (see Figure 2-1). The difference is they are offered resources and support from leadership to help them succeed. They can see a clear path to help them move forward.

Unproductive pushing leads to stress, whereas productive pushing paves the way for tension. Without any kind of a push, organizations remain stagnant. A company needs three elements to turn stress into tension: a vision of the ideal state, a clear grasp and hatred of the current reality, and the right skills,

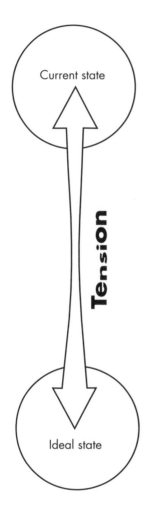

Figure 2-1. To create tension a leader must have a vision of the ideal state, a clear grasp and hatred of the current reality, and the right skills, capability, and actions to close the gap between the two.

capability, and actions to close the gap between the two. The leader is responsible to provide all three elements. If any of them are missing, no matter how powerful the remaining forces, productive tension will not be created.

Being visionary is different than creating a vision of the ideal state. Most visions have two major faults. For one, they are often directed to the wrong audience. Most leaders can not recite their company's vision. When they are asked about the company's vision, they commonly steer persons to the lobby wall. Those visions are for customers, not the company. They provide a comforting feeling for customers, containing good marketing jargon like "committed to our customers" and "world-class quality." The second flaw with most visions is that they simply state the outcome. Anyone can create an ideal state that includes perfect quality, perfect delivery, or increased market share and profits. This is not an ideal state, it is simply "good stuff." An ideal state should provide an image of how the organization should function.

It should not be easy to reach consensus about a company's ideal state; a vision should challenge people to see a different potential, to choose a different path, or to develop a clear path.

An ideal state provides a direction. The ideal state does not need to be pared down into a single paragraph that fits on a poster. It should live in employees' hearts and minds, and pepper their everyday conversations. Here is a snippet of a good example of one company's ideal state: "We strive to provide ease of ownership—easy to buy, easy to own, easy to maintain, easy to use."

Ideal states are not necessarily the same for everyone within an organization. The ideal state for a customer service representative should relate to his or her work. The same goes for a salesperson, a machine operator, an accountant, and so on. Every person, function, and process should have an ideal state. This is not to suggest that companies create a dozen three-ring binders filled with ideal state documents. Ideal states are not pieces of paper, but ongoing dialogues that take place as leaders teach, coach, and encourage workers every day.

To provide a compass for the journey, the participants in a lean transformation must have a clear sense of where they are currently as well the ideal state to which they are heading. Lean leaders need to help everyone understand the current reality and instill a hatred of the condition. They must articulate the current problems, gaps, and opportunities. They must understand their relevance to the big picture and long-term success, and determine the root causes of the conditions. Most leaders have great difficulty dealing with current reality. They convince themselves that they fully understand the issue and develop a false sense of security. For example, knowing current numbers is important, but it does not indicate a grasp of the current state.

While some people believe it is difficult to develop a hatred for the current state, it is really not that hard. Take a group of people on a waste walk, and they will begin to see opportunities. Have employees focus on what leaves them frustrated at the end of the day, and they will see opportunities. Even the most financially successful companies are filled with people who are disgusted with the current condition. But, they believe that have no control over the current condition. This brings to light the third element of creating tension: presenting a clear path forward.

After they create clear pictures of the ideal and current states, leaders cannot passively hope that people are compelled to act. The leader must choose the path that will lead from here to there and create a vehicle to drive change. This includes giving people the right skills and knowledge to close the gap and making some tough decisions about things like organizational structure. Leaders do not need to give people a minute-by-minute script. But if they do not provide any direction, everyone will look at the chasm that needs to be crossed and at each other to see who is going to take action. Everyone might have his or her own idea about how to cross the chasm, but nobody will take a running leap if he or she does not believe that everyone else is following. The leader must pull people together (through consensus or dictatorship) and provide the means to cross the chasm.

## LEADERSHIP MOVE THREE: ELIMINATE FEAR AND COMFORT

A lean culture requires action, experimentation, and new thinking. For many organizations, these activities involve risk. Most organizations, even those known to be innovators and risk-takers in the marketplace, are typically risk-averse internally. A lean leader must create the right environment to encourage and force experimentation. Leaders need to eliminate the fear associated with such activities and likewise the comfort that exists in maintaining the status quo.

Individual and collective learning only occurs when people step out of their comfort zones—the set of conditions and activities with which they are familiar and under which they know how to operate (see Figure 2-2). Comfort zones provide people with safe havens from all of the changes about which they think they have no control. They know what needs to be done and what results they are going to get because they have done the task many times before. A lean leader must eliminate the com-

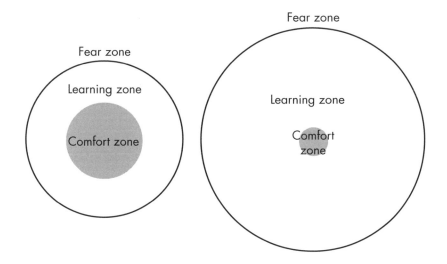

Figure 2-2. Learning only occurs when people step out of their comfort zones.

fort zone and direct people to the learning zone. For people to learn, they must step outside the bounds of what they currently know. They must change the conditions and rules under which they operate. This does not mean chaos and unorganized change. Stepping out of the comfort zone should be purposeful, continuous, and multi-dimensional. The leader must force people out of the comfort zone by setting clear goals and providing mechanisms. It is not simply about setting higher targets. It is requiring individuals and organizations to experiment purposefully. A leader should not reward those who hit the numbers by merely repeating everything they did the year before.

Leaders can use every operational review, coaching session, and conversation to coax, prod, and push people out of their comfort zones. If a leader asks a worker every day about the experiments he or she has performed toward improvement, the worker will eventually have to conduct some experiments to answer the questions.

In addition to eliminating the comfort zone, the lean leader must eliminate fear. If people step too far outside of their comfort zones, they enter fear zones. To eliminate fear, leaders must provide safety in three distinct forms: physical safety, emotional safety, and professional safety. Physical safety may seem like an obvious necessity, but leaders must ensure that people and the environment in which they work are physically safe before asking them to try new things.

A person who brings forward a new idea in a staff meeting, and is immediately ridiculed, will think twice before speaking out again. A lean leader must squelch such criticism and provide emotional safety. Attacks often come in subtle, passive-aggressive forms, but the leader must address them head-on. If an individual is punished for trying something new that fails, whether it be by something as innocuous as receiving a bad review or as serious as getting fired, everyone will get the message that failure should be avoided at all costs—even at the expense of not improving. While someone who repeats the same mistakes should be disciplined, the person who takes risks and learns from them should be rewarded.

Another way a lean leader can eliminate fear and move people out of their comfort zones is to model the proper behavior. Many leaders model "knower" behavior instead of "learner" behavior. They create false impressions that they know nearly everything. Knower leaders hide gaps in their knowledge as they consider them signs of weakness. People see through this. They have much greater respect for a leader with integrity, someone who knows his or her limits and is willing to become vulnerable by moving out of the comfort zone. When a leader demonstrates the "knower" persona, everyone copies that behavior as a path for promotion. Learner leaders, on the other hand, acknowledge their failures and publicly learn from them. This often throws people off the first time it happens, because most people do not expose their failures (and instead hope nobody notices).

Building creative tension is not a one-time, organizational-wide event. It is an everyday behavior. It is not based on slogans or posters, but on dialogue and coaching. It is not featured in brochures, but in actions. Leadership has the responsibility to build genuine tension, not to fake crises or impart veiled threats.

## LEADERSHIP MOVE FOUR: LEAD THROUGH VISIBLE PARTICIPATION, NOT PROCLAMATION

Perhaps the greatest falsehood in change management is the myth of "management buy-in." When different levels of a company are asked if they have management's commitment, they inevitably respond, "Oh yeah, we have their buy-in. They are 100% behind this." Being "behind" an initiative is quite different than being in front of it, however. A major element of a lean manufacturing process is pulling product through the process, not pushing it through. Change management is the same. The leader must be pulling the organization through the change process, not pushing it through. When a leader is pushing, the organization's people do not know if they are being pushed toward something better or off a cliff—they do not have this concern if leaders are out in front and pulling.

Too many leaders think that by allocating resources, attending some reporting sessions, and writing a few company-wide e-mails, they have done their part in leading lean. That may be enough for a new product launch, a fundraising campaign, or a new computer system, but it is not enough for cultural and operational transformation. A leader can not write a proclamation that the organization will become lean and expect people to automatically adopt new practices and different ways of thinking. Management buy-in must eventually turn into leadership commitment or the organization will never reach its full potential.

What does commitment look like? Think: active engagement. Are leaders participating in activities that transform the organization or are they watching from the sidelines? Leaders often believe they do not have the time to commit to active participation. They think it is sufficient to proclaim the importance of lean. As the adage goes, "Actions speak louder than words." The ways leaders spend their time influence the organization's priorities. People watch, some purposefully, others uncon-sciously, the everyday actions of leaders. If an organization's leaders spend their time on financial reviews, presentations, status reports, and decision-making, its people will mimic those priorities. If leaders participate in (or ideally lead) kaizens, waste walks, and five why problem-solving coaching, then people within the organization will understand that lean warrants priority status. If "not enough time" is the leader's excuse for not participating in lean, then everyone at the company will cite a lack of time as well. If in reading this you think that you really will not have time, participation in lean does *not* mean micro-management. It does mean coaching, side-by-side engage-ment, encouragement, and support.

Setting a good example is not the only reason to actively participate in lean. By participating, leaders directly observe how lean is being understood (or not understood) and applied. Seeing people solving problems, identifying and eliminating waste, and working with teams tells a leader more about the lean transformation's current state than reports, walk-throughs, and secondhand stories.

## LEADERSHIP MOVE FIVE: BUILD LEAN INTO PERSONAL PRACTICE

Most people, particularly leaders, view lean as something that applies to others, not something that can help them be-come better managers and leaders. This is a critical mistake. Instead, leaders need to take a good look at their own practices, starting with standardization. They should develop clearly struc-tured processes for how they perform certain activities, and design a structured flow for how they spend their time during the week. They need to make improvements and use them to become more predictable, while eliminating waste and surfac-ing problems or gaps as they occur. For example, if there is a structure for your week, does it go out the window on Monday because of something unforeseen? Why does the issue (or is-sues) that pops up interfere with your process? Should some-one else handle the problem? Can you eliminate the problem?

Do you have an unrealistic schedule? Standardization, despite its sound, is not static. It is dynamic and changes based on conditions, needs, and improvements.

Leaders should build on standardization with learning, or the scientific method. They need to make decisions, solve problems, and deliver improvements with a more deliberate sense of what they hope to accomplish. Suppose there is an improvement idea to reallocate some resources out of quality and back into line management. The scientific method would begin with a hypothesis, which is a critical link and the lynchpin for learning. The hypothesis in this case might be: by making line management more responsible for quality, 50% more defects will be found in-process versus inspection. The hypothesis can be tested as the plan is developed and executed. In testing the result, the valuable information gained helps learning. Was the hypothesis correct? If 50% is exceeded, what was missed in the observation? The scientific method and process improvement are at the heart of a lean culture.

A leader must also commit time to reflection. Reflection should not just be for the sake of looking back, but looking back to learn what was most effective and then looking forward to decide what should be done. The organization should take time to work on improving itself, and the leader must improve himself or herself as well.

Leaders and managers will become more effective by aggressively applying lean to their job functions. If the scientific method is used to help make improvements, vital tasks will be performed more effectively. There will be a learning curve for leaders, but also for those they are trying to lead. Applying lean to the leaders' and managers' job functions conveys legitimacy upon lean efforts, methods, and principles. It is a more powerful vote of confidence in lean than simply writing an endorsement letter. It is important for leaders to broadcast their incorporation of lean to those around them. Leaders should do the five whys on a whiteboard, not $3 \times 5$ cards, for example.

## CONCLUSION

To teach, a leader has to learn, and learning lean is more than a cerebral exercise. Concepts need to be applied. Otherwise, a leader might be able to read a few slides on lean, but he or she will not be able to coach people on how to apply lean thinking on a daily basis. Leaders must be teachers. By applying lean to everything (including coaching efforts), a leader will become a more effective teacher.

Remember what leadership is really about: it is not a job; it is an act. Anyone can be a leader. But in assuming this role, a person has to learn how to teach, to build creative tension, and to eliminate fear and comfort. He or she must actively participate in the transformation of the business and apply lean to his or her own job. A lean leader needs to carefully consider these leadership attributes and responsibilities. As a leader, imagine you have a customer attached to your hip all day. What would that customer say about how much value you provide to them? Customers only value a leader's ability to bring about change, to bring the organization forward toward the ideal state. What would your customer say? Reflect upon these questions as you plan your lean journey.

---

### Five Leadership Moves for Lean

1. Leaders must be teachers

2. Build tension, not stress

3. Eliminate fear and comfort

4. Lead through visible participation, not proclamation

5. Build lean into personal practice

---

# 3

# Learning Can Be Expensive: Five Common Lean Pitfalls (and How to Avoid Them)

Lean transformation success takes more than doing things right. It is also about avoiding pitfalls that can lead to failure, whether outright failure or simply a failure to reach full potential. Cultural and process changes can be very complicated, and wrong turns can set a company back months or even years. The authors have witnessed many failures. Mistakes are made to be learned from, not hidden. This chapter outlines the five most common areas of failure.

Failure can wear many disguises. At its most innocuous, failure may indicate that an organization falls well short of its potential, despite its apparent lean success. Many companies fit this definition, achieving compounding returns on their efforts yet never coming close to the robust success of Toyota. Other companies fail by making false steps that delay any significant progress. These companies often go through cycles, repeating mistakes and eventually clawing back toward positive momentum. Some organizations fail in more spectacular and fatal fashion, such as one company that was so focused on "internal lean" that it forgot to sell its products.

The five common lean pitfalls that follow can occur at any point in the lean transformation. Avoiding them at the start of the journey will not guarantee success. Leaders must always be on the lookout for signs of lean failure, just as they should always be on the lookout for organizational arrogance, complacency, or risk aversion.

## PITFALL ONE: BELIEVING LEAN IS ONLY ABOUT MANUFACTURING

The myth of Pitfall One is common. However, many articles and stories describe companies that "break out" of manufacturing and apply lean elsewhere in the organization. This is typically portrayed as an amazing revelation for companies that achieve this breakthrough. But the message is decades old. Taiichi Ohno, considered the founding father of the Toyota Production System, once said, "The Toyota Production System is not just a production system." Very early on, Toyota integrated design, suppliers, and the customer, mostly out of necessity. Toyota's early financial situation was so bleak that banks would not loan it capital to build cars until it had orders in hand. To get beyond this constraint, the company had to improve its whole process, not just manufacturing. To this day, Toyota continues to expand beyond its traditional boundaries, bringing lean to its dealers through its Signature program, which is based on waste elimination, the five whys, and process improvement.

A chief concern about Pitfall One is that companies are not always focused on the right problems. As a simple but clear example, if manufacturing lead time is reduced to 12 hours but order entry takes two weeks, customers will not be any happier. There seem to be three dominant reasons why people get stuck in the lean-equals-manufacturing mindset. The first is that there is an abundance of media, books, and training focused on "lean manufacturing." Obviously, the assumption is that lean is all about manufacturing. This has a self-reinforcing effect, where one person learns lean manufacturing from another and then goes on to write his or her own article about lean manufacturing, perpetuating the myth that lean is a manufacturing tool. This has perpetuated to such an extent that people wonder whether lean *assembly* will work in a machine shop—but the machine shop is precisely where Taiichi Ohno conducted his first experiments and refined lean transformation.

A second reason people equate lean with manufacturing is that manufacturing is the most visible and measurable part of the organization. Upon walking through a plant that is in the midst of lean transformation, it can be seen whether or not there have been improvements. Pictures can be taken of the results of Five S and kanban cards and they can be shown to others, declaring "this is lean." It is easy to measure manufacturing and, while often the wrong things are measured, every manufacturing manager has at least a dozen numbers he or she can recite to explain process performance. A manufacturing plant may make improvements to increase productivity, but that does not necessarily mean its controller has improved the efficiency of closing the company's books.

The third and final reason for this mindset is because a company often starts its lean transformation in manufacturing (and rightly so, since this is often where most money is spent), so all other functions immediately associate lean with manufacturing. Other functional leaders see manufacturing's efforts to break lean out of manufacturing as an attempt to encroach on their territory. Even though the concepts were identical, one multi-billion-dollar company changed the lingo of the training materials it used outside of manufacturing so its training did not appear to be manufacturing-based.

When manufacturing does start to convince those outside of manufacturing that lean applies to them, it often takes the wrong approach, further complicating matters. Manufacturing folks see how much waste other functions create in *their* processes; to them, lean in design, finance, sales, and other areas is about eliminating the waste those functions cause in manufacturing. Design and engineering should design products that are easier to manufacture. Sales should provide a more even and level flow of orders. But the people in manufacturing fail to realize that manufacturing is *not* the customer. The customer pays a company for its products or services. Suggestions from manufacturing may help a company get closer to delivering value to its customers, but the suggestions should be framed as what is best for the customer, and not manufacturing. Sure, companies can view manufacturing as an internal customer of designs from engineering. But internal customers need to take a back seat to external, *real* customers. How can this common trap be avoided? First, frame everything from lean training to action plans in terms of how there will be more value delivered with less waste to external customers. Keeping this frame of reference front and center provides an effective check against some of the distortions in purpose that will occur. This point of reference should be repeated constantly. Most companies should maintain this perspective regardless of any problems they may confront.

Second, lean efforts can be started somewhere other than manufacturing or at least in a non-manufacturing area simultaneously. A large gas and electric utility began lean in finance. This made it clear to everyone that lean was not just about plants, and created living examples of lean transactional processes. If a company has already begun its lean journey in manufacturing, it can move to a non-manufacturing area, and use that as the jumping-off point for the rest of the organization.

Third, strike the term "lean manufacturing" and use as the latter word "thinking," "enterprise," "systems," or another phrase instead. The use of "lean manufacturing in finance" does not do anything to break down the wall. And, as lean is trained and communicated, the focus should not be just on manufacturing tools such as andon cords and kanban cards; lean rules and principles should be presented as the foundation that will apply to any process.

## PITFALL TWO: THE LEAN DEPARTMENT SHOULD NOT BE LEADING LEAN

Here is a review of the differences between leadership and management. *Management* maintains current reality. Current reality does not plod along all by itself. It requires coordination, problem solving, and decision making. *Leadership*, in contrast, moves companies and departments toward the ideal state. So while a lean department might play an active role in managing lean, it should not be leading lean.

Full-time lean resources might use any number of names: lean promotion office, continuous improvement department, or lean champions to name a few. And those individuals heading up such groups could report to anybody from the CEO to a shift manager. Having a dedicated lean department is not vital; many companies have successful lean programs without one. However, the establishment of a dedicated lean department is recommended. A company pursuing lean transformation still needs to deal with day-to-day, minute-by-minute firefighting— things that could interfere with the lean journey. Even mighty Toyota, after half a century of lean, still dedicates resources to promote and develop the Toyota Production System.

Once a company appoints a lean manager, however, the immediate effect is predictable; most leaders in the organization abdicate responsibility for lean transformation to the manager. There is a precedent for this organizational behavior: safety managers take over responsibility for safety from all the individuals who can actually do something about it, while quality managers assume responsibility for quality so everyone else can focus on getting the products out the door. The logic is obviously flawed, yet it is surprising how often this happens.

So if the lean manager is not responsible for lean, who is? The quick answer is *everyone*. In a lean organization, everybody has a lean coach—his or her immediate supervisor or boss. Team leaders coach team members, and group leaders coach team leaders. This is the *primary* responsibility of each individual—not signing time cards, filling out evaluations, or signing off on requisitions. Each plant manager, department director, and vice president should own the lean strategy. There is a risk that all of the strategies could become disconnected, but there are better ways to handle this than by turning lean entirely over to the lean manager. Whether the coordinating mechanism is the CEO, a lean steering committee, or hoshin/policy deployment, if the leaders are not responsible for the lean strategy, then several potential problems could develop into significant risks.

One possible problem is that the lean strategy could become isolated and serve itself, instead of being connected to the business goals and strategy. If a company creates its lean strategy in isolation, it will likely execute it that way as well. Another stumbling block is that leaders might not buy in or commit to lean. Most organizations report that they have leadership commitment; however, leadership's commitment often only extends to endorsing the plan and signing the checks for the resources. This is not commitment. Commitment takes personal involvement to make it happen. Commitment requires removing barriers. Commitment means getting your hands dirty. Saying "yes" is too easily confused with true commitment. And turning over the lean transformation strategy to a lean manager is one of the first ways to engender fake commitment.

So, if the lean manager and his department are not responsible for the lean strategy, what should they be doing? The answer depends on where the company is on its journey. In the early stages, the job is one-quarter education (combining training and coaching), one-quarter coordination and communication, and one-half pushing a rope. While leadership commitment is necessary, the lean department can play a vital role in moving the effort forward until people are ready to pull for help. Down the road, as the lean culture of the organization matures, the lean department can become involved more in coaching than teaching. They also can help ensure that lean progress continues (and raise red flags when it is not), build new connections across and outside the organization as needed, and then . . . get out of the way. Peoples' roles in the lean department change from that of creators to stewards, from enforcers to supporters, and from actors to observers.

How can the common trap of turning over lean to the lean department be avoided? First, and perhaps most simply, clear roles and responsibilities must be created before putting the resources in place. Do not wait for the organization to break into bad habits; instead, the lean department's tone should be set early on as a resource and a catalyst for new activities, not a surrogate for leaders. Second, simple and structured mechanisms for the interactions between the lean department and the leaders must be created. This forces leaders to stay involved, whether they truly own the lean strategy yet or not, and creates alignment with the lean department. Third, it should be ensured that the lean department is two steps ahead of everyone else in understanding lean. If the department does not have to struggle to keep up and understand where the organization should be going, it can ensure that things are not heading in the wrong direction. Fourth, no matter how effective and convenient it might be, the lean department should not become the primary architects of the lean strategy. When the departments' people act as problem-solvers and implementers, they are the only ones learning lean. They prevent the organization from taking responsibility. The lean department certainly can facilitate and coach, but if it becomes the head, hands, and feet of lean, these important features are amputated from the rest of the organization. Leaders must *lead*.

## PITFALL THREE: ACTIVITY SHOULD NOT BE CONFUSED WITH PRODUCTIVITY

Many components of a lean journey require a lot of activity: training, steering team meetings, benchmarking, and study. These activities can consume vast resources and make those involved feel upbeat about their roles in making lean happen. None of these activities produces results, however. The only truly value-added activities in a lean program are those that directly deliver results—those that change the process or fix a problem.

Value added, in the strict definition of the phrase, requires three criteria:

1. The customer must value it and be willing to pay for it.

2. It must change the product or service.

3. It must be done right the first time.

Real value-added activities actually work on the product or service. The business of lean transformation is . . . transformation. If lean activities do not produce results that improve the organization for its customers, shareholders, and employees, then they are not value added.

A company should consider whether non-value-added activities are necessary and determine how they connect with or support the value-added activities. Training is a popular, and absolutely necessary, activity. Without training, people do not know what to do or how to do it. Training is a major weapon in a company's arsenal of change. If a company trains its people on the wrong material at the wrong time in the wrong way, this would be unproductive and wasteful. It would be well-disguised waste, however. "We're training everyone on lean," the progress reports might note. Who could argue with that? If a company does not enable its employees to create change, does not give them enough or the right skills to create change effectively, or does not develop any mechanisms for change into which they can plug themselves, its training may have been better left sitting on the shelf. One Fortune 25 company trained its entire workforce on lean basics, but when it failed to devise mechanisms for the employees to walk away from their moving assembly line to work on improvements, the effort yielded little to no results. The training led the employees to believe that lean was the beginning of something good, and they waited to hear more from management. Management sat back and waited for the employees to take the ball. Nothing happened, and the company was on the verge of wasting years of investment.

Some companies confuse activity with productivity when they measure the wrong things during lean efforts. Partially at the encouragement of several consultants and books, many companies measure the percentage of employees trained in lean and the percentage of employees who have participated in kaizen workshops. In this scheme, companies celebrate plant managers, whose percentages are higher than their peers, as committed to the success of lean. But companies typically do not review whether this actually produces results.

Lean is not alone—companies often do not apply action orientation to a number of activities including leadership development and strategic planning. Meetings, research, and discussions are necessary, but only if they support action. There are dangers on the flip side of this issue when a company values results at all costs or covets today's successes at the expense of tomorrow's. Anyone can squeeze a few more dollars by starving an organization of needed development, investment, or improvement. Or an organization can temporarily ramp up production to an unsustainable level. A company's leaders should resist the urge to swing the pendulum too far in this direction. Attention must be paid to results and processes, achievements and behaviors, and the ends and the means.

There are two primary levers to help companies avoid confusing activity with productivity. One is the scientific method, a concept built into lean itself but rarely followed by leadership. The scientific method refers to the process of developing a hypothesis, or being able to state the effect expected based on the cause or action taken. If a department rolls out detailed training plans, what result does it expect to achieve? If a kaizen is planned, what result is anticipated? "Results" can not always be quantitative, and that is fine. The important question is, "Has the outcome from the action been thought through?" Financial managers ask this question all the time, sometimes expecting an overly detailed return-on-investment calculation for each investment they make (even if they fabricate the numbers). Clarity during hypothesis planning forces people to be more deliberate about the specific actions they must take to achieve specified outcomes.

A company can also apply more focus. In an operations review, the focus is mostly on two things: broad aggregate results and future plans. Rarely do executives ask to be shown past plans. Companies make the assumption—wrongly—that if the plans were right, the aggregate results should be good, and if the aggregate results were poor, then the actions or plans were wrong. Many variables can affect aggregate results; therefore, a company should never use aggregate results as a basis for decision-making, coaching, or future planning.

Proper coaching and teaching can only take place when leaders get close enough to observe the actual work people perform— not by reviewing aggregate data and obscure plans. Getting in the trenches focuses necessary attention on the value-added work that makes change happen. And continual assessment and coaching allows leaders to build their knowledge and capabilities.

## PITFALL FOUR: EVENT LEAN PREVENTS A COMPANY FROM BECOMING GENUINELY LEAN

Several years ago, a Tier 1 automotive supplier in Michigan was promoted in a series of billboards that said "14,751 kaizens and counting," or something in that ballpark. This began the company's promotion about its lean journey and kaizen events. It also began a round of event-driven lean in the auto industry. The company featured in the billboards failed to produce sustainable results, although it did produce tremendous short-term results.

Outsiders to the operation, either contractors or internal consultants, predominately lead and plan event lean. A company reports event lean results separately and distinctly from operational results. And its leaders discuss event lean within the organization as if it is an entity that people can touch. This highlights a fundamental problem: event lean is separate, distinct, and disconnected, and never becomes an integral part of an organization. A company is doomed to play catch-up by staging enough lean events to drive out the waste it produces from actual operations.

Early on in a company's lean efforts, event lean can be successful. It is visible because it is markedly different. Event lean delivers results because it is highly structured to do so. But genuine lean is absent. Genuine lean cannot be distinguished from how companies operate because . . . it is how companies operate. Genuine lean is built into an organization's culture, people, planning, problem-solving—everything its people do, touch, or say. A company can not create genuine lean overnight, and may, in fact, need event lean to help get it there. But too much reliance on event lean prevents a company from achieving genuine lean.

Why is event lean bad? After all, it does produce results. Undesirably, organizations create a pattern of turning lean on and off like a light switch. This leads to a barrier that prevents the daily integration of lean. It also means that if lean can be turned off, it can remain off for an extended period. A company that gets stuck in event lean has a tremendous tendency, when times get tough, to back off or stop lean efforts. Because a lean event takes some investment in time and resources, managers think they can hold off on the investment until conditions improve. Meanwhile, skills and momentum get stale, waste creeps back in, and cynicism about management's commitment becomes a legitimate barrier. Few companies that turn the lean switch off for awhile can easily turn it back on again.

Another reason event lean is bad is that it only engages some of the employees some of the time. In an assessment of one Kansas company's lean efforts it was discovered that the assembly area had not had a kaizen event in nine months. Kaizen was the dominant form of lean in the company. However, since an event had not been planned in such a long time, employees in the assembly area believed lean was over. They had not seen lean in nine months and management had no idea of the problem because it was busy with lean in another area of the organization.

Lean is like a muscle; the more it is used, the stronger it grows. Conversely, if an employee only experiences a lean event every few months, he or she has no chance to strengthen the muscle and it begins to atrophy. Because a company is really investing in the skills and capacity of the organization to create change, event lean does not yield progressive results. Each event strains unused muscles again and again, and the organization never grows stronger and never reaches the next plateau.

How can a company avoid getting trapped by the event lean pitfall? First, it should create a small but living model of genuine lean early. This may not contribute major results to the bottom line right away. The model is meant to be small and, to a degree, isolated—a Lean Learning Laboratory$^{TM}$. In essence, what is created is a small team of people who are centered on a common process. They essentially have to work together and build lean principles, practices, skills, and tools into their team.

This living model can develop into a standard against which to compare the rest of the organization.

An event lean cycle also can be avoided by assessing the results well after a lean event is held. At some organizations, it makes sense to re-review the results of a kaizen one week, one month, and three months after the event is held. After one week there is usually some deterioration in the new process; after three months, it may be completely wiped out. The problem is that lean events do not leave new lean thinking or skills behind, and old thinking recreates old processes over time. Instead of measuring and rewarding people based on results they achieve on the day of a lean event, measurements and rewards should be based on the results posted three months after the event. This ensures that managers pay attention to the cultivation of a lean culture and capability as well as the short-term achievements of the lean event.

A third way to ensure event lean becomes genuine lean is to role model the behavior. Managers are comfortable with their event lean roles—they sponsor the event and show up on Friday to congratulate the team. Managers should not be allowed to stay in this false commitment pattern. They should be models of lean, visibly using its principles and practices to solve everyday problems, make everyday decisions, and contribute to tomorrow's performance. Setting this pattern at the management level creates the right example for everyone else in the organization.

## PITFALL FIVE: TORTOISE LEAN WILL BEAT HARE LEAN

Everyone remembers Aesop's timeless fable of the tortoise and the hare, portrayed more recently by everyone's favorite hare, Bugs Bunny. The faster hare jumps ahead to an early lead in the race, becomes overconfident and lazy, and gets trounced by the tortoise who maintains his purpose and pace over the long haul. The same lesson applies to lean. Those who rush out of the gate toward the finish line without any understanding, respect, or attention to the entire race will run out of steam far too early and lose in the end.

Sprinting toward the finish line of lean without realizing it is a never-ending marathon can cause a company to plateau early and veer away from its destination. A hare-like approach can also create new barriers that prevent organizations from kicking it into high gear for a second sprint. A common question of leaders is, "How long will it take my company to become lean?" When told it is a journey that never ends, the inevitable response is, "I know, but how long?" When an organization sees lean as a destination instead of a journey, it typically seeks quick solutions. Instead of a lean transformation, it dashes toward the finish line in a flurry of andon cords and kanban cards.

One large company, wanting to see how far and fast their plants were getting to lean, devised a lean audit. It had every lean tool imaginable, including standard work instructions, andon, kanban cards, and Five S. The company evaluated the plants' levels of proficiency and generated a series of scores. Senior leadership admonished plant managers with low scores and told them the company would find someone else to lead lean if their numbers did not improve. Not surprisingly, the managers quickly found ways to succeed in the audits. Everything looked great on paper, but nobody knew the true purpose of Five S; the company was not truly on a path to lean. The moral of the story: the second a company puts a stake in the ground and says, "This is the finish line," people will find a way to reach it. But if they do not understand the journey, they will never truly enter the lean race.

Instead of ruminating about things that give the appearance of progress, a company's leaders should focus on the seeds that will help it grow into a robust, lean organization. This does not mean that a company should expect to invest for three years without any payback and then hit the jackpot in year four. It does mean that every time standard work instructions are developed, more structured activities are built at the management level. Every kaizen held helps others learn the power and skill of directly observing work. Every error-proofing process leads to another informal five-why analysis. Attention must be paid to the less tangible elements of lean that will become the true lean foundation. The foundation can not be assessed with a check-the-box process. People must be observed as they are doing their work—value-added work, the work of management, and the work of improvement.

An observer might find disappointment in the lean tour upon walking the aisles and taking pictures of a company that is beginning to build a solid lean foundation. An observer may not see the most structured Five S program, spotless floors, or andon lights going off. But employees will voice how they are always trying new things and continually trying to improve processes so they are safer, more efficient, and produce higher quality. It is easier to build the tools into a solid foundation than it is to build a new foundation on top of a bunch of lean tools.

## CONCLUSION

The five lean pitfalls explored in this chapter are not the only ways companies can fail. For example, a company might train the wrong people at the wrong time on the wrong stuff. Or the company may tackle problems that are not critical to the business. It could change strategy every three months and never make any progress. A company's leaders and its people must be committed to the lean journey. They must be on the lookout for potential problems and be prepared to raise the flag or pull the andon cord. A company's leaders should not wait for the pitfalls' consequences to wreak havoc before taking action. If there is a decline in operational performance, disengaged employees, cynicism, and confusion, it is too late. No lean journey will be perfect. The most successful organizations learn, adjust, and adapt along the way.

## Five Common Lean Pitfalls

1. Believing lean is only about manufacturing

2. The lean department should not be leading lean

3. Activity should not be confused with productivity

4. Event lean prevents a company from becoming genuinely lean

5. Tortoise lean will beat hare lean

# A Thousand-step Journey: Five Phases of the Transformation Roadmap

Roadmaps, despite some drivers' aversions to them, help to guide people on their trips. Dumb luck can sometimes get travelers headed in the right direction (and often in the woefully wrong direction), but a roadmap sure helps the process. A roadmap will prove invaluable to a company during its lean journey. In this chapter, a lean transformation roadmap is constructed through five phases including the areas of concern—from education to infrastructure.

The map will not prescribe the exact route a company should take, but it will help demarcate the journey and suggest options. The choices made will depend on a company's unique set of conditions and criteria. Some of the considerations influencing the path taken include:

- where a company is before it begins lean transformation;
- what conditions or issues it is dealing with through each phase of the trip; and
- the company's willingness and ability to adapt and change based on the actual experiences and learning of its workers.

The lean transformation roadmap includes five phases, but the lines between each phase are typically blurred, and the characteristics can blend together. It is important to understand that the roadmap can be viewed from the department, plant, or company level. One part of an organization might be at one phase, while other parts, or even the entire organization, are at a different phase.

A word of caution is offered: make sure the appropriate amount of time and resources are devoted to lean transformation. It may be difficult to believe, but there are organizations that have put less time into planning their lean journey than the time you will spend reading this book. This is a surefire prescription for failure and an exercise in futility. Do justice to the lean journey.

## WHAT LEAN IS—AND IS NOT

Before exploring the lean transformation roadmap, it is important to step back and review the concept of lean systems development. There are a couple of prevailing misconceptions that must be highlighted and dispelled.

### Misconception: Lean is About Tools
### Reality: Lean is About Systems

First, "Lean is *not* about tools!" This is a common misunderstanding. Many people and organizations view lean as an assorted collection of tools. This limited view of lean is the single biggest contributing factor to lean transformation failures. Unfortunately, more companies fail (or do not reach their potential) than succeed on their lean journeys. The failure rate is disappointing. Companies should beware of anyone trying to preach and implement lean as kaizens, Five S, total productive maintenance (TPM), or some other collection of tools.

Lean systems require an understanding of the *thinking* of lean—a company's leadership needs to recognize the purpose of what it is trying to achieve to select the appropriate tool. This requires an evaluation element, such as performance measurements, to reflect achievements and drive the appropriate behavior. Internal systems (information technology, human resources, etc.) are required to connect the organization together.

It is the combination of tools, evaluation, internal connections, and lean thinking that form a lean system—and lean thinking is at the core.

## Misconception: Lean is a Finite Goal
## Reality: Lean is a Journey

Question: When will a company be lean? Answer: *never*. It is a mistake to think there will be some endpoint where a company will proclaim that it is lean, dismantle all of the lean systems, and return to business as usual. A company may become leaner, but if it is truly lean, the journey will never end. When thinking lean, there will always be a gap between where the company is (current state) and where it would like to be (ideal state). Therefore, there will always be opportunities to improve. Proclaiming that a company is lean will only serve to draw a line in the sand and effectively stop any forward progress.

Of course, successes should be proclaimed along the way—to recognize and reinforce behaviors and accomplishments. But true success will be achieved when the organization continues to move forward at such a pace and with such a passion that it is difficult to slow it down and it is impossible to stop, regardless of how well it is performing.

Toyota recorded a $10.4 billion profit in the same year it reduced operating expenses by $2 billion. Toyota is a company that, by most people's standards, is lean. It is a good thing Toyota does not think that way. Its approach never changes: Toyota always focuses on the ideal state, and it executes that approach better every year.

## LEAN TRANSFORMATION EVALUATION CRITERIA

Lean is a way of *thinking*. It is a journey that is *never* over. It is a system framed in a collection of rules and principles. Before starting the lean journey, a company must consider where it is right now. Current conditions and criteria must be examined. Some of the following 10 criteria may be more important than others to consider at the different phases of lean transformation.

## 1. Tension

Typically, tension carries a negative connotation. It is associated with headaches and difficult circumstances. When a company is pursuing lean, however, tension is a good thing. In fact, the urgency for lean and its introduction into an organization is always easier when a company is struggling—when there is sufficient tension—than when it is doing well. The real challenge is to get organizations to embrace lean in good times.

To develop tension, not stress (stress arises out of hopelessness), a company needs to develop and articulate a clear vision of the ideal state's characteristics. Then it must contrast that against a deep understanding of its current state and define the gap. It does not matter how well a company is performing because there is *always* a gap. The gap creates the tension.

For example, to instill some tension and a sense of urgency for introducing lean, a presentation was given to the senior leadership and management staff of a building materials manufacturer. After hours of discussion, it was clear the presenter failed. The company was experiencing healthy profit margins; its market share was growing; and it was practically debt-free. It was not until the company's ideal state was defined and its leaders witnessed choreographed plant tours to reveal the current state that they recognized the gap. The tension was immediate and the leaders' response was decisive.

## 2. Go for the Pull

If tension helps spur momentum for lean, it is best to capitalize on that momentum by engaging champions predisposed to recognize the tension. An entire company cannot be taken on all at once. So, start where there is a "pull" for lean rather than trying to "push" it in another area. Most organizations start lean in their production areas where the effort is highly visible and likely to reap the most benefits. However, when determining where to start, it is often best to evaluate where there is the greatest pull. Look for a champion, sponsor, or compelling business need.

As an example, a major gas and electric utility company started its lean efforts in the finance area, because that is where the champion and the pull existed. Lean eventually spread to its power plants, service centers, and other parts of the company.

## 3. Leadership Involvement

There are no better champions and no better advocates for pull than a company's leaders. It is ideal to have senior leadership actively engaged in the lean journey, not just sitting in a seat, but also driving the vehicle. Unfortunately, senior leadership typically delegates the responsibility of guiding the lean journey to others of lesser authority.

Even though there was a sponsor in the gas and electric utility's ranks, it was difficult to engage senior leadership on the journey in the early stage. To implement and institutionalize lean, activities and structures at the management level were developed. This elevated the value and results of lean to senior leaders, and today they are active and effective in leading the utility on its lean journey.

## 4. Business Conditions

Business performance will determine what "gear" a company is in as it moves forward in its lean journey. If a company is in survival mode or is under extreme pressure to immediately improve performance, then leadership should focus on the immediate application of lean tools such as kaizens, waste elimination, or Five S. Development of a lean culture may be put on the back burner for better times. If the climate is competitive pressure and recognition of the need to improve, a company should begin with the tools but in parallel, work on changing the culture to sustain and continue the improvements. If a company is in a growing, flourishing industry that is facing little pressure, then it should work specifically on developing the lean culture and apply the tools as a manifestation of the culture.

## 5. Baggage

"Baggage," refers to the bad taste left by past unsuccessful organizational initiatives. A company often overlooks this when it begins to design a lean approach. It does not make any difference if the baggage is real or perceived; it should not be ignored. Baggage may include past corporate initiative activities that resulted in layoffs or failed to satisfy expectations. It may also encompass the "flavor-of-the-month" syndrome. The organization's people may be primed to "wait it out or wear it out" until the latest initiative—lean transformation—fades as well.

## 6. Culture

Consider the cultural makeup of a company. "Culture," does not refer to the "lean culture" to which a company may aspire. Rather, it is the unique traits and characteristics of the people within the organization. Are there particular sensitivities to consider, such as language? For example, multilingual training and development materials may need to be offered. There also may be literacy issues. For example, at an aerospace supplier some basic lean tools were presented in expectation of significant results as the company had many ripe improvement opportunities. After less-than-stellar results, it was realized that there were some basic reading and math deficiencies to address.

## 7. Resources

Ideally, a company will want the resources available to develop and dedicate certified lean specialists to the business units, plants, or specific areas. "Certified" means they are proven to have reached some specified level of proficiency as determined by the company. The importance of this is to establish a common language and a common lens for those who are driving the organization. The specialists can act as internal consultants to teach, facilitate, and help direct lean efforts. However, competition for resources or the relative size of the company may result in the addition of lean to someone's current responsibilities. Regardless, resource availability or constraints must be considered when designing the approach.

## 8. Integration

More often than not, a company introduces lean either during or after other continuous improvement initiatives. This can cause confusion between initiatives such as lean and six sigma. One should not replace the other; they should complement one another.

One lean implementer likes to explain lean as, "...the systems you need to fight the daily fights and manage the war. Six sigma, on the other hand, is the tool you need to storm the beach." No matter how it is looked at, an organization must see lean as a complement to the initiatives in which it is engaged. Lean must be perceived as the vehicle to take an organization to new heights. Successful efforts should not be negated. Lean should be used to leverage a company's effective efforts—not replace them.

## 9. Measurement/Evaluation

Measurement/evaluation systems dramatically influence organizational behaviors. Unfortunately, the resulting behaviors often conflict with the desired behaviors of a lean initiative. A company should carefully look at what it measures and evaluates, and who is accountable.

At a major automotive parts supplier, direct labor was the Holy Grail: "drive out direct labor and you will be rewarded." The easiest way to drive out direct labor was to automate processes, so that is what the company did. After closer examination, however, the company's leaders realized that costs actually increased because of downtime, scrap, indirect support, inventory, and other issues. The point is not that automation does not have a place in lean; it absolutely does. The point is the measurement drove the behavior, which is not the best lean practice.

## 10. Vocabulary

Vocabulary may seem like an unimportant consideration, but jargon can be confusing. Employees of organizations become increasingly confused as leadership introduces one initiative after another—the flavor of the month. If a company has a "process excellence" initiative, the title should not be changed. Instead, it should be integrated with the rules, principles, and practices of lean. If a lean concept is introduced, but there is already an existing word with the same meaning, keep using the same word.

## THE TRANSFORMATION ROADMAP

As previously mentioned, the roadmap consists of five phases with common elements, but different approaches within each phase (see Figure 4-1). The roadmap will help assess what phase a company is in on its lean journey and what needs to be considered at each phase. Remember, the lines between the phases will be blurred, and it is likely a company will not neatly fit into one phase. Each phase focuses on some common elements: education, application, communication, infrastructure, time frame, tools and methodology, and expected results.

### Phase Zero: Exploration

It may sound strange to begin at "zero," but there is a reason. Not all businesses need to experience the exploration phase. Those organizations already committed to lean often skip it and proceed directly to Phase One. Some companies, however, may need to assess whether lean is appropriate, where it is appropriate, and how to start. Typically, leadership and/or management initiates Phase Zero by trying to understand more about lean, how it might fit into the organization, what challenges it may pose and, most significantly, what payback it may offer.

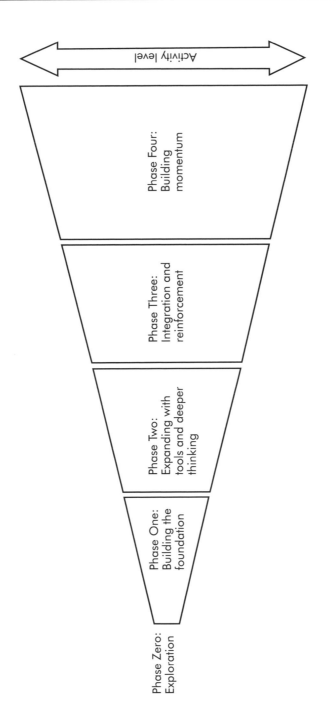

Figure 4-1. Shown are the five phases of the lean roadmap.

## Education

In Phase Zero, an organization develops an awareness and general understanding of the application and benefits of lean. An organization may also assess its current state to identify its lean education gap. These efforts help a company evaluate lean's "fit." Usually, those within the organization who have initiated the inquiry about lean, or their delegates, participate in the educational process. Although it may include seminars, conferences, networking, or benchmarking, there is typically very little education, in the traditional sense, during Phase Zero. Often, the focus is more on simple tasks such as reading or benchmarking visits.

## Application

Except for a bit of dabbling, companies typically do not apply lean tools or techniques during Phase Zero. In fact, it is discouraged. Without a solid background, efforts could result in failure and sabotage of the program before it gets off the ground. This happens often. A company latches onto a particular tool, gives it a try, and fails. The tool might have failed because of poor implementation or simply because it was the wrong tool for the organization. Regardless, the result is "lean is not for us." Imagine a hospital investigating lean and trying to apply "takt" time to the emergency room or U-shaped cells to the surgery rooms. Those specific tools would not work, but the hospital could still reap tremendous benefits from lean.

## Communication

There is no formal communication during Phase Zero, but it is likely that a "rumor mill" emerges from the exploration. Leaders should be prepared to respond to questions about the company's plans for lean and to allay any fears about its implications. Even in this early exploration phase, caution should be exercised to manage the expectations.

## Infrastructure

Essentially there is no lean infrastructure in Phase Zero. There are probably a handful of people in the organization investigating lean and assessing its application. They may be engaged in some reporting and sit on a decision-making team, but that is about all.

## Time Frame: 0 to Approximately 6 Months

If a company is already committed to lean, it can skip Phase Zero. Otherwise, the time taken to explore may take several months, but not a year or more. If Phase Zero is extended into a year or longer, a company usually experiences a void in leadership and an absence of tension. An effective exploration of lean can be easily completed in 0–6 months if given the available resources.

## Tools and Methods

The application of lean tools is discouraged during Phase Zero. However, companies commonly try some tools, such as:

- kaizen workshops,
- Five S, and
- kanban.

The application of tools at this point will likely appear disjointed and lack purpose. Often, because of its misguided application, a tool can become the organization's definition of lean and can short-circuit the transformation process. Kanban can be particularly dangerous during Phase Zero, because a company has not sufficiently established process stability, and thus it does not recognize the power and potential of the tool. It is crucial to understand that lean is *not* about a tool or even a set of tools. It is about systems, thinking, and understanding of purpose.

## Results

Little-to-no performance gain should be expected during Phase Zero, except for possible "event" gains from a kaizen.

What is gained is a clear understanding of lean, recognition of its potential, and an awareness of its challenges.

## Phase One: Building the Foundation

Phase One assumes that a company has explored lean as outlined in Phase Zero, and a decision has been made to move forward with lean implementation. The company is ready to embark on the journey; now its leaders need to figure out how to navigate the road ahead.

Lean applies to every type of industry as long as companies understand that lean is a way of thinking and about rules and principles—not a collection of tools. A company that mistakenly equates lean with tools deems lean inappropriate if the tools do not fit its business. The company's leaders need to first understand the rules and principles of lean and then identify the best tools for its industry—ones that will manifest lean thinking.

The lean transformation roadmap applies, regardless of industry. Organizations representing automotive and aerospace manufacturing, healthcare, electric and gas utilities, food processing, automotive dealerships, electronics, medical devices, consumer goods, and other industries have successfully adopted the roadmap.

To establish the lean foundation, a company will engage in a surface application of basic lean tools and begin to establish a lean culture by developing rules and principles. In Phase One, a consensus is reached—that lean is about the way business is done and not a series of events or projects.

In Phase One, a company's leaders will also begin to understand and apply tools to uncover the true current state and build tension in the organization. It is critical for an organization to recognize tension so it can embrace the potential of lean. Tension will be helpful at every step of the lean journey. It can be used to drive the smallest of activities all the way to the vision of the business. Beware: there are some organizations that, once the gap is exposed, relieve tension by lowering the vision of the ideal state or inflating the current state. If a company is performing well, or at least performing well against its own standard or an industry benchmark, the issue of tension needs to be carefully considered to discover how to foster it. If a company simply closes the gap between its current reality and its ideal state without making any real changes, all energy for making future changes will be lost.

## Education

In Phase One, education begins in earnest. Those who take critical leadership and implementation roles in this early state develop a deep understanding and appreciation of lean's rules and principles. These persons come to a realization that lean tools act as a countermeasure to problems and as vehicles that reveal lean thinking. The focus is primarily on basic tools.

To develop lean tool skills, it is helpful to apply the "learn, apply, reflect" approach:

- Learn—provide the training and expose participants to the need for the tools and implementation techniques.
- Apply—transfer learning immediately to participants' areas where they can test and apply the newfound knowledge. Always recognize the potential for improvement.
- Reflect—review the effectiveness of the application and validate the internalization. Continue to implement successful strategies; make modifications in areas where improvement is needed.

## Application

Application is an important component of Phase One as well as all subsequent phases. Here, organizations typically focus on one or many small areas. To illustrate, a food processing company with multiple plants started its lean transformation in a single small area in each plant. However, the focus was on a different area in each plant. For example, one plant chose maintenance, while another selected product processing. This enabled the company to learn from different areas. Primarily, the application tests the effectiveness of various basic lean tools and engages the organization in small, yet meaningful and highly visible improvement activities. Application at this phase also helps organizations evaluate response and provides feedback to assess continuing implementation plans. During its lean journey, a company will invariably revise and refresh its implementation plan. Application in this phase is more about learning and cultural change than it is about breakthrough results.

## Communication

An organization in Phase One uses communication to build a "burning platform," a clear and powerful reason to change, and spread the message of lean's importance and value. Regardless of whether the company is in dire straits or on top of the heap, a clearly articulated message of why change is needed must be crafted. Faking a crisis will quickly dissolve effort and ruin leadership credibility. The company's potential is articulated by leadership, providing insight into where the lean transformation journey is heading. It is critically important to manage expectations. This is one of the major challenges during the journey and, if not addressed during Phase One, it becomes increasingly difficult to manage in later phases. The old adage, "under-promise and over-deliver" serves an organization well in this early stage. Statements from employees such as, "We're moving too fast," "It's going too slow," "It does not apply to our area of the organization," and "I do not see any results" are sure indicators that businesses have not done well in managing expectations.

While the message about lean needs to be consistent, communication can take many forms in Phase One. Existing channels, such as newsletters, town hall meetings, bulletin boards, and other formal mechanisms can be used. One effective approach is to develop a "cascading" communication plan where the message cascades through each level of the company starting with the CEO down to the shop floor. The only caution with cascading, as with any direct person-to-person communication, is to ensure the message does not get diluted or filtered to suit the messenger.

## Infrastructure

A company has an infrastructure to manage its business. It also needs to develop an infrastructure to manage lean implementation. In Phase One, the efforts focus more on clarifying roles and assigning specific responsibilities than on building formal hierarchies. The infrastructure is dependent on the existing resources or those made available. External resources can be of great benefit.

Some of the questions a company's leaders ask in Phase One include:

- Should we commit full-time resources and designate a lean specialist?
- Should we build an internal lean group competency?
- Do we centralize or decentralize the lean expertise?
- What do we want our management oversight to look like?

Additionally, an organization needs to establish clear goals and metrics as lean targets. The infrastructure will evolve over time as more resources become available and the lean expertise of the business matures.

## Time Frame: Approximately 3–9 Months

Phase One should not take more than a year, even in the most resource-constrained organization. If a company's leadership has not established a solid foothold for lean and demonstrated measurable results within the first year, organizational support will wane and attentions will focus elsewhere. There are exceptions; a medical device manufacturer wanted to establish the culture as a first-year goal and was less concerned with its metrics.

## Tools and Methods

Tools in Phase One have three primary objectives:

1. Stabilize operations for testing and experimentation.
2. Provide the foundation for sustained learning and the internalization of lean thinking.

3. Achieve measurable results to realize a solid return on investment.

Some of the tools to consider include:

- waste walks,
- kaizen events,
- learning laboratories,
- Five S,
- visual management, and
- standardization.

How to execute waste walks should be one of the first, if not the first, lean skills an organization develops, even before Five S (which is often first). This allows a company to identify opportunities for improvement, observe current reality, and understand and appreciate the other tools. For instance, a company will appreciate Five S as far more powerful than just a housekeeping tool if it recognizes the tool's potential for waste elimination.

As for the other tools, a combination is recommended, some implemented in parallel and others in series. For example, a kaizen event can achieve rapid measurable results while learning laboratories can act as living organisms that instill lean skills and thinking in a small part of the organization. The parallel application of these techniques satisfies the three primary objectives outlined previously.

## Results

In Phase One, a company should base results on measurable performance improvement and use this to establish a foundation for the cultural transformation. If a company needs to quickly demonstrate strong performance gains, it can develop kaizen events or move to Phase Two right away. If a company goes this latter route, however, there will not be a proper foundation, which will likely adversely affect lean implementation later on.

Typically, a company localizes performance gains and uses fairly standard metrics: safety, quality, delivery, and cost.

Broader metrics like lead-time probably do not figure in Phase One. An organization should use results to examine and assess the effectiveness of the internalization. Has lean "stuck?" Are behaviors changing? Are the rules and principles vocalized?

Reflection may play a role and can be very beneficial. Periodically ask: What was supposed to happen? What did happen? What should be institutionalized? What should the company do differently?

## Phase Two: Expanding with Tools and Deeper Thinking

In Phase Zero, the applicability of lean under certain business conditions was investigated, along with what should be considered to move forward. In Phase One, the decision was made to move forward. Now the company's leaders need to develop implementation strategies.

Up to this point, the approach has focused on the surface application of basic lean tools in a small, but clearly defined part(s) of an organization. Phase Two expands lean to a larger part of the organization and burrows deeper into lean tools and lean thinking. The focus is now on critical business issues, not just localized issues and opportunities.

### *Leadership Engagement*

At this point in the journey, organizations should have acquired a strong appetite for lean. It may not be pervasive, but it should certainly occur in pockets throughout the company. To prove the value of lean, an organization needs to demonstrate success. To spread the word, it needs prophets. A company can probably get to this point without much leadership engagement. However, Phase Two requires active leadership involvement, including specific and well-defined direction.

In Phase Two, the lean journey is all-encompassing: it infiltrates and makes an impact on most of the organization. The "organizational needle" on the overall performance gage needs to move. All stakeholders need to recognize lean's impact. Expanding the focus, however, complicates lean's implementation and exposes an organization to more obstacles. An active leadership, one that understands lean's critical business issues, can help overcome obstacles.

Instituting change is like pushing a large, heavy flywheel to build momentum (Collins 2001). It takes a lot of effort to get it moving; over a period of time, however, it builds its own momentum. A company needs to keep pushing the wheel and building momentum. Without leadership involvement, obstacles slow the momentum and even more effort is required to continue. The goal is to get the wheel moving on its own so obstacles and barriers can not slow or stop it.

One major public gas and electric utility was able to make huge gains in localized areas like its service centers and power plants. However, as the complex organization attempted to expand the lean focus and application, it met one obstacle after another. Regardless of the obstacles' authenticity, the utility could no longer overcome them with brute force or localized lean successes. It needed help. Once the CEO, two presidents, and a gang of vice presidents got actively engaged, it was remarkable how many of the obstacles simply disappeared. Additionally, the lack of alignment and connection with the utility's goals and objectives and its proposed lean activities was surprising. An organization can not gain alignment and connection (policy deployment), without understanding its leadership's expectations and without leadership's active direction.

## Education

In Phase Two, an organization needs to expand its lean education efforts. It should build deeper skills and across a wider cross-section of the company to deal with tough problems and capitalize on bigger opportunities. In Phase One it was inch-wide and foot-deep. In Phase Two, it is mile-wide and mile-deep. It is equally important for an organization to educate its senior leadership. Leaders can not effectively direct and engage in what they do not understand. Leaders do not have to know precisely how to use the tools. But they need to understand lean rules and principles and recognize the tools' purposes.

Education in this phase should focus on internalizing lean thinking as well as lean tools and techniques. An organization in Phase Two should use the language and behaviors that reflect lean thinking. This phase is as much about cultural change as it is about operational change.

A Lean Learning Laboratory™ or L3 is the most effective technique available today for developing lean skills and internalizing lean thinking. Since L3s should be an integral component throughout the lean journey, a review of the concept is provided here.

Simply put, an L3 is a place determined by a process, subprocess, or geography; it is a place in which to experiment, learn, practice, and apply lean ideas, concepts, and tools at a faster pace with less risk and with a greater frequency than throughout an entire business unit. An L3 includes a small group of people in a highly visible area of the organization who successfully learn and apply lean's rules, principles, and tools, and who serve as a catalyst for broader application of lean throughout the business unit. Usually L3s start in production areas, but they are just as applicable in business offices as they are on production floors. A Chicago manufacturer of construction products instituted its first two learning labs in the customer service area and the roll-forming production process.

L3s are not events. Like the lean journey itself, they do not have end dates. They are living, dynamic organisms that continue to develop people's skills and expand influence. The labs typically include 5–20 people, who include experts and managers from the defined area, upstream and downstream process representatives, and internal supplier representatives. For example, a major dairy products company established its first L3 in the butter churn area. The lab team included day-to-day operators (subject matter experts), a supervisor, representatives from milk operations and packaging operations (upstream and downstream operators), and preventive maintenance (PM), quality, and production scheduling (internal suppliers) personnel.

Training and development of L3 team members can vary, but a company should incorporate two key strategies. First, it is recommended to use the "learn, apply, and reflect" approach: the group is trained on a new lean skill; the newly learned skill is applied in the laboratory area; and the group reflects on the application's effectiveness and internalization of the skill before moving on to the next training topic. Second, lean teams need to train the group on basic lean tools to stabilize the operation before introducing more advanced tools. For example, an L3 should not start with kanban of one-piece flow until measurements are in place. Further, an organization should have mechanisms, such as Five S, to systematically eliminate waste and surface problems, which will establish a stable platform upon which to build.

Once it has established an L3 in one area, and it is satisfied with the approach and effectiveness of application of the lean concept, a company can start another lab in another area. Ultimately, a company should have many labs in many different areas at the same time. Each lab may be at a different level of lean maturity, but they all should be going in the same direction and learning from each other. People from a mature lab in one area may "seed" the start of a new lab in another area.

Following are some basic requirements for L3 success:

- Establish a realistic schedule to meet the organization's commitment to the laboratories.
- Establish a laboratory huddle and team-meeting expectations.
- Dedicate time and materials to allow laboratory teams to perform their intended functions.
- Ensure the active participation of all support functions in sustaining the L3s.
- Build early management review (auditing) into the implementation schedule. Use the plan-do-check-act cycle approach.
- Expand L3s throughout the organization in a timely manner.
- Measure the progress of L3s and their impact on organizational performance.
- Ensure processes are consistent among shifts and labs.

- Use training modules that are based on organizational needs and that will present opportunities for verifiable success.
- Develop training that includes application and repetition for internalization.
- Design a well-defined, decision-making structure.

It is important to have a solid understanding of the L3 approach and its implementation before a company moves into Phase Two, the expansion and focus of the lean journey.

## Application

The small, localized areas that have already started on the lean journey should move to the next plateau by applying more advanced lean tools and developing mechanisms and structures to sustain performance gains. Much of the application from Phase One should now be standardized. A company needs to capture lessons learned and apply them more broadly to all areas of the organization. Also, the application of lean should focus and align more with key business issues—those critical process/performance opportunities that will generate significant measurable gains. Application is no longer in one area of a plant or plants. It is moving into every area of the organization based on a well-planned implementation approach. The application of lean in this phase is far more directive and less ad hoc than in Phase One.

## Communication

Communication should continue to build upon the message from Phase One: recognizing the importance and value of lean. A company should use communication to focus on lean's tangible results and share best practices. Communication should provide direction or act as a compass, deploying clear goals and metrics throughout the organization. The metrics should be as predictive as possible and focused on strategic objectives and desirable outcomes versus rearview mirror results. Among the most effective means of communication are one-on-one meetings between those people who have already started on the journey and those who are about to begin. A company can leverage informal communications with a formal structure. It can dedicate specific times for learning circles in which people can share information. As is the case along any point in this journey, a company should be cautious about managing expectations. It should not over-promise future commitments or artificially inflate past results.

## Infrastructure

The lean infrastructure a company develops is based on available resources and leadership commitment. At the very least, an organization should clearly define lean roles and responsibilities, and some key operational leaders should drive education and execution. Individuals should be identified as the organization's internal lean specialists or consultants. These individuals may be part of a centralized lean group, within an operating unit, or both.

During Phase Two, the major public gas and electric utility developed its lean specialists and provided support from a centralized group. However, at some point in the development process, as capabilities evolved, the utility shifted the specialists into various business units.

A company should also consider and develop a lean oversight structure, such as a steering or management committee. This group should include senior leadership and key operational leaders who are responsible for assessing progress and providing direction.

## Time Frame: Approximately Six Months to Two Years

As with all phases, a variety of variables affects the timing for Phase Two. What resources will the organization commit? Is leadership actively engaged? Have early initiatives been successful and demonstrated measurable results? Is the direction clear and aligned with goals throughout the organization? The answers to these questions and the confluence of other variables will determine the time frame.

As a general guideline, companies should be in Phase Two for six months and up to two years. To illustrate an exception, however, lean implementation at a major automotive supplier was very much a "lead up" initiative. Key operational leaders and management pushed lean up to the senior leadership group. The senior leaders supported lean when they could see the return. But they did not understand its rules and principles; they did not provide specific direction; and they were not proactively engaged. It took more than three years before the supplier could convert the "push" from management to a "pull" from leadership.

## Tools and Methods

In Phase One, a company focuses on the application of basic lean tools in a localized area. In Phase Two, there are three avenues for application.

1. In localized areas where stability has been achieved, the focus is expanded beyond the basic tools such as Five S, waste elimination, and work instructions to more advanced tools such as kanban, just-in-time (JIT), and quality alert systems.
2. Areas that have yet to begin applying tools can begin by expanding on the basics from Phase One.
3. To provide a more enterprise-wide application, a company can use value stream mapping to identify opportunities and hoshin planning to focus and align everyone in the organization toward the same destination.

In Phase Two, it is likely that project teams using lean thinking may begin to tackle larger areas, processes, or problems that provide a wider enterprise impact than those a kaizen workshop can handle.

## Results

Phase Two focuses 25% on building knowledge and 75% on performance results. A company should expect some breakthrough results that start to move the organizational performance needle. Focus areas from Phase One should sustain gains and consistently improve performance based upon an agreed set of aligned metrics. Expanded focus areas should start generating measurable results at a more rapid pace than in Phase One because of a company's accelerated learning curve. Measurements are critical in Phase Two. Not only do they need to align and clearly connect to organizational goals, but they need to influence the development of lean behaviors in the workforce. Performance measurements have a strong impact on the behavior of the workforce.

## Phase Three: Integration and Reinforcement

In Phase Three, a company integrates lean into every aspect of its businesses. This phase assumes a company has stabilized lean processes and behaviors. The goal is to integrate lean into every activity so it becomes a natural part of day-to-day operations. Lean should be the fabric of the organization. It is what holds people, processes, and products together and dictates how an organization manages its daily activities. At this point, lean implementation should be stable enough to handle any person, process, or problem as a matter of routine.

Moving from Phase Two into Phase Three requires assimilation of two key points.

1. Leadership is critical. Managers maintain current reality. Leaders move the company and its people toward the ideal state. Harry S. Truman once said, "Leadership is the ability to get men to do what they do not want to do and like it."

   Phase Three is more about leadership than it is about tools. Leadership does not necessarily refer to a position or rank. What is a "leader?" Leaders, regardless of their official titles, move an organization forward and are influential, respected, mindful, and caring. Lean proponents must look for leaders at every level of the enterprise. Leaders may not be ready to embrace lean, so a company's lean champions need to convince them with action, not words.

Remember, lean is about transforming *thinking*. Leaders must be able to teach and coach to make an impact on thinking. Leaders can not lead if they can not teach; and they can not teach if they are not willing to learn. Teaching and coaching involve more than just preaching or making speeches. They require a deeper investment in people. Winston Churchill once said, "Telling is an act. Coaching is making a personal investment in someone."

Leaders must overcome an organization's natural resistance to change. To accomplish this, they require three things:

A. Leaders must have a firm grasp of the current reality and a true distaste of remaining there.

B. Leaders must have and be able to articulate a vision of the ideal state.

C. Leaders must have the courage to tackle closing the gap.

2. Focus on the problems. As companies transition into Phase Three, small everyday problems become more evident. This is the objective. Problems should not be viewed as embarrassing, but embraced as opportunities to improve.

Typically, organizations tend to focus on serious mishaps. However, in one study it was shown that for every serious adverse event, there were 10 less serious adverse events, 100 almost adverse events or near misses, and 1,000 contributing factors to those events. A company should not focus exclusively on the "big" problems if it does not know which of the 1,000 small problems might create the big problem. Leaders can not solve all 1,000 problems. Instead, a company needs everyone sensitized to small problems and skilled in dealing with them so they can solve the daily problems that generate unfavorable results and lead to bigger predicaments. An organization can not do this by focusing on top 10 lists. Mechanisms and skills must be in place to bring problems to the surface and allow for their resolution.

## Education

In Phase Three, education should continue to build in scope and depth. Everyone in the organization should have a basic level of understanding, a common language, and a fundamental skill set. With this common ground, sense of unity, and clarity of purpose, communication is easier and more effective.

Based on their positions or skill in applying lean principles, practices, and techniques, a company should confer the title of lean "master" onto some individuals. These masters should demonstrate the ability to apply, with consistent success, all lean tools. They should also exhibit lean behaviors in every aspect of their day-to-day activities. Most importantly, they need to have the ability to teach and coach other individuals in the organization and to recognize high-potential candidates for the lean master ranks.

Lean instruction is no longer a separate or standalone channel of education; it is integrated into other existing channels, possibly as a regular part of supervisor development or new employee orientation. One of the reasons for Toyota's success is it embeds Toyota Production System instruction into every learning opportunity for all employees starting with their orientations and extending into every facet of their work throughout their careers.

## Application

During Phase Three, organizations should incorporate application of lean into all areas and all functions of a department or location and validate it with measurable results. Simply moving lean into new areas is no longer sufficient. Expanding in this phase means manifesting results that are measurable and indicative of continual improvement in conjunction with the daily exhibition of the desired behavior. This will not happen at the same time in all areas of an organization.

Functional areas, departments, locations, and facilities will likely be in different individual phases of the lean journey depending on where they started and their pace of development. However, by Phase Three in the overall organization, no department, function, or location should be untouched. The application of event-driven tools—kaizens, six sigma, or demonstration projects—will continue to play a major role. However, much of the application should begin to shift from these forced, facilitated events toward natural and conscious behaviors and activities in the day-to-day business operations.

It should seem as if all individuals are wearing glasses with the same lens, allowing them to see and react similarly to daily lean principle opportunities. From CEOs to supervisors to shop floor stewards, everyone should use common language, exhibit comparable behaviors, and provide the same kinds of guidance. Application is now seamless and routine instead of piecemeal and orchestrated.

## Communication

The formal communication channels developed in prior phases should continue. However, there is more informal person-to-person or person-to-team communication during Phase Three. A company can establish communication channels outside its walls as well—with stakeholders, for example.

## Infrastructure

Depending on resources, a company relies on either a centralized lean group or local lean specialists for its internal infrastructure. The roles of the lean group and specialists change in Phase Three, however. Area leaders within the organization should start to assume responsibility from the lean teams for implementing lean transition. The lean group should shift more to coordination, support, and coaching than implementation. A company should be cautious, however. Responsibility should not be transferred until skills have been developed. To do that, build processes to encourage and facilitate transition.

At one snack food company, there were a number of activities being conducted in the name of lean. However, it was found that these efforts were not connected to the specific goals and objectives of the organization. In Phase Three, every action a company takes should have a specific purpose based on leadership's guidance and direction.

## Time Frame: Dependent on Variables

It is difficult to assign a time frame to Phase Three. Ideally, major pockets within an organization should spend less than two years in this phase. However, Phase Three could take another year or so. At approximately two years into the journey, the areas that first implemented lean should be assessed to determine their progress. At this point, lean should manage the day-to-day business and continuous improvement should be self-directed.

As part of lean implementation, periodic lean assessments of the entire organization are recommended. These assessments are valuable to stimulate reflection on progress and provide direction. In some cases, an organization or parts of an organization are numerically scored on progress to compare against the ideal state and provide a baseline for future assessments.

## Tools and Methods

An organization continues to use the tools introduced in the earlier phases. However, additional and more advanced tools are required in Phase Three. Although it may seem obvious that an organization should always understand the purpose of the tools and methods it employs, it is surprising how few organizations recognize their intent.

For instance, it is common for people to think the purpose of Five S is "housekeeping." This could not be more off the mark. Housekeeping and an organized workplace are the *results* of Five S. But, the *purpose* is to make problems immediately evident.

A similar misunderstanding exists regarding pull systems. The common belief is that they are designed to "control inventory." In reality, their purpose is to simply and specifically connect a supplier and a customer, internally or externally.

An organization should design and implement tools in Phase Three to satisfy two specific purposes. First, standardization should be created up, down, and across the company. A very powerful, but not very well known tool to help accomplish this is control point standardization (CPS). It is generally accepted that standardization of daily activities applies to the shop floor or to employees in repetitive, transactional type processes. It is assumed that standardization does not apply to managers. However, CPS helps organizations recognize that all of its workers, regardless of position, have certain control points and certain things that should be done at regular intervals. Each person requires standardized activities to ensure each control point is addressed. The more variable the activities, the more difficult they are to standardize. But there are always control points. CPS is typically started with supervisors and moved up to managers. Sometimes it is even extended to senior leadership.

Second, an organization should use tools to develop integrated systems that connect the entire company. For example, many people are familiar with a quality management system (QMS) that integrates quality across an organization. However, at this point in the journey, it is recommended that a company seriously consider the development of an operating system—a system that integrates business operations across the entire organization. This system connects the organization together around common tools, common metrics, common internal systems (like QMS), and common principles (thinking) so all are headed in the same direction.

Many companies say they have an operating system, but most do not. The authors of this book have worked on the development of numerous operating systems and have made many mistakes along the way. This has given us the ability to recognize a real system when we see one. As an example of a failure, at one company we developed what we called an operating system. It was a checklist that required neither any real thinking nor any real leadership. It was simply connecting the dots of a well-designed framework on a piece of paper. In fact, the paper became the system. When the senior leadership of this company left, so did the system, which means it was not really a system.

## Results

At the end of Phase Three, an organization is building upon already-found gains. It is experiencing major breakthroughs and its performance is moving forward at a constant pace. Some areas of the organization begin to differentiate themselves from the rest of the organization. And, the organization differentiates itself from its competition.

## Phase Four: Building Momentum

In Phase Three, the goal was to integrate lean practices and principles into every facet of the organization to the extent that lean becomes the DNA of the organization's existence. In this, the final and perpetual phase, a company focuses on continually reinforcing lean and maintaining momentum.

When an organization reaches Phase Four, there is some danger it may fail to recognize lean is a journey that is never complete. Because the company experiences constant breakthroughs in performance, its leaders and workers may become complacent and even arrogant. In this never-ending phase, a company must constantly reinforce the rules and principles of lean. It must develop an insatiable appetite for continuous learning. Failure to pursue learning as a core competency may lead to a spectacular downfall.

Many of the Phase Four characteristics do not differ significantly from Phase Three—except for intensity, depth, and duration.

## Lean is Evolutionary

Lean is not a one- or two-quarter transformation. It can take one or two years—longer, even—just to build the momentum for this never-ending journey. There are many lean tools that deliver fast and significant results. But, if a company does not internalize the principles of lean, improvements will slowly deteriorate or plateau at a level far below the organization's potential.

Such a long-range commitment often serves as a barrier, particularly in public companies whose journey may be interrupted by short-term interests such as the need to satisfy external expectations. When objectives conflict, it is often easy to abandon lean efforts in some misguided belief that lean is an expense and not an investment. This hampers immediate efforts to improve organizational performance, and also makes it twice as difficult to reenergize a lean initiative in better times.

## There will be Mistakes

The authors have been involved in many lean implementations in companies of all sizes and industries. We have yet to see implementation go as planned or as expected because "stuff happens." Although proper planning is critical and poor planning guarantees poor execution, perfect planning does not guarantee perfect results. It is impossible to anticipate every contingency. There will be surprises. Outcomes will not be as expected; and unforeseen obstacles will be encountered. The key is to accept that there will be mistakes—and not to repeat the same ones.

Here are a couple of points to ponder during implementation. First, focus on what can be controlled and influenced. The low-carbohydrate fad has been a powerful external influence on the snack food industry. There was little manufacturers could do when consumers jumped onto the low-carbohydrate bandwagon en masse. Instead of whining about the things they could not control, they should have focused on what they could control, such as operations or product development.

Second, a company should be willing to take chances and test things. There are many opportunities to test tools, test approaches, and test techniques. Too many are lost to presumptions such as, "It will not work in our industry," or "We can not do that in our area."

## Education

Education is the cornerstone upon which lean will continue to grow and develop. It helps keep everyone sharp and focused, and serves as a beacon for ideal states in every aspect of a company. Education, therefore, should be an ongoing series of opportunities to learn formally—such as through seminars, workshops, and benchmarking—and informally. Informal education takes place through coaching, mentoring, and organizational scans. It is critically important to recognize that leadership must promote, encourage, and practice both formal and informal avenues of learning.

## Application

Lean is now not only integrated into every day-to-day activity in the organization, but is fully integrated into every decision-making thought process. The principles and practices of lean should be woven into the collective thinking of the organization—just as your principles are woven into your individual thinking.

## Communication

In Phase Four, a company should be communicating about lean externally with suppliers, customers, financial institutions—even the community. Communication takes on new meaning and purpose. The goal now is to engage others as well as inform them. Communication in this phase should also serve as a vehicle to recognize and acknowledge employees' contributions to the company's success.

## Infrastructure

At this point in the journey, lean skills and infrastructure are embedded in the organization of every business unit, regardless of the service or product provided. Roles and responsibilities are clear and standardized at every level of the line organization. There likely is still some semblance of a centralized lean group, but it is now focused primarily on assessing the organization to identify gaps and barriers to the continued lean transformation. Management provides direction and guidance and ensures accountability. The expectation is that the lean group is now mostly a resource for the oversight group and not involved in line management.

### Time Frame: Ongoing

Phase Four is the easiest phase to assign a time to—it does not end. As long as management and leadership maintain the commitment and the organization continues to learn, progress will continue.

### Tools and Methods

By Phase Four, a company has used and internalized every lean tool and methodology applicable to its industry. The goal now is not to acquire more tools, but to develop a mechanism that aligns and connects the organization's goals with the most effective and efficient application of tools. An organization should not undertake any corrective action or improvement initiative unless it can be clearly and obviously connected to its goals and objectives. Hoshin planning or policy deployment must be used to integrate the company's goals and objectives throughout the organization at every level.

### Results

Lean efforts and culture drive performance gains in safety, quality, cost, delivery—even brand value. The benefits at Phase Four of lean transformation not only affect performance; they affect the strategy and tactics the company employs to compete in the marketplace.

## REFERENCE

Collins, James C. 2001. *Good to Great: Why Some Companies Make the Leap—and Others Don't*. New York: Harper Business.

**Five Phases of the Transformation Roadmap**

0. Exploration

1. Building the foundation

2. Expanding with tools and deeper thinking

3. Integration and reinforcement

4. Building momentum

**5**

# Pulling it All Together: Five Dimensions of an Operating System

Lean is not tools. Nor is it systems or principles. It is not metrics or value stream maps or customer satisfaction. Lean is not any one thing; it is how everything works together. That is at the heart of an operating system, which will be explained in this chapter, along with its five dimensions. Lean is not implemented; it is a journey. An operating system is the culmination of the effort, and understanding how a company's operating system works is crucial to making lean a part of it.

Can you cogently describe *how* your organization operates? Beyond simple one-word adjectives such as "chaotic" or "effective," it is difficult to articulate how a company runs its business. Yet the hallmark of any world-class organization is an ingrained system to coordinate actions, execute daily work routines, learn, and make improvements—in short, its operating system. In these organizations (and hopefully yours too), the operating system is the engine that drives the company.

Many companies look for a silver bullet. They jump on the latest quality fad, the newest improvement program, or the best employee engagement practice. A company's leaders frantically benchmark the organization and magically appear to be making immediate and remarkable improvements. They attempt to distill their efforts and create a program to adopt the new approach. Despite their best intentions, they never realize the broad, sweeping improvements they had expected. Does this sound familiar?

Adopting new tools and new methods, even those that appear wildly effective in isolation, is insufficient. Organizations also need to build a consistent, comprehensive system that provides context and structure to operations on a daily basis—one that will accommodate improvements on an ongoing basis. All world-class companies have built their own unique operating system. Your company should develop one as well.

## WHAT IS AN OPERATING SYSTEM?

As shown in Figure 5-1, the framework of an operating system integrates:

1. Principles (to align thinking and build culture);

2. Systems (to process vital work, outline the way work gets done, and connect the organization);

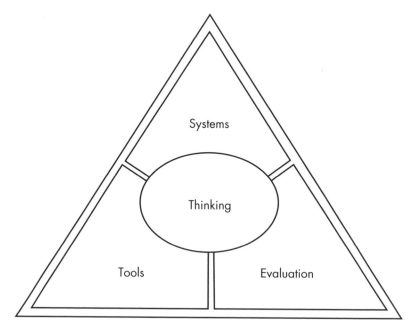

*Figure 5-1. The framework of an operating system is illustrated.*

3. Tools (to generate new approaches and execute the thinking); and

4. Evaluation (to understand where the company is against where it wants to be in the future).

These four elements incorporate a critical fifth dimension: consistency. Taken together, the elements create a common way of thinking, operating, and improving the business. They also establish a standard set of practices for all employees.

An operating system is among the most misunderstood concepts in business today. When the authors of this book are on-site and ask for help identifying operating systems, companies often point them in a number of directions including the IT department (no, this discussion has nothing to do with computers), a list of lean or six-sigma tools, organizational structures, and mission and vision statements. While each of these individual pieces is important, they must all be connected as parts of a much larger system.

## AN OPERATING SYSTEM ALIGNS "HOW" WITH "WHAT"

To create alignment, coordination, and understanding, companies must create a shared agreement about *what* they plan to accomplish (goals, metrics, targets, and strategies, for example) and *how* to operate (such as methods, processes, and practices) to achieve the objectives.

Forming consensus about what to do is critical, since failure to do so leads to an organization without direction. Fortunately, most companies spend considerable time and effort creating agreement about goals and objectives; unfortunately, the conversation typically ends there. Each department is left to its own devices to move from the current state to the target state. In the worst cases, departments move in directions counter to one another.

An operating system is the process through which a company reaches agreement about how to operate and improve. It is how objectives and tactics are executed day in and day out. An operating system creates the infrastructure and framework for employees to use to reach the company's collective target state.

Consider a football team. Good teams establish goals before they face their opponents, such as number of turnovers, number of points required, and number of points yielded to the opponent. However, coaches do not send 11 random players onto the field to improvise during the game. They do not defer to each player to find his own way to win. Coaches develop offensive and defensive philosophies and test associated playbooks. Regrettably, most businesses do not take the time to design and communicate their playbooks. It is the operating system that makes truly great teams and great players, not the other way around.

## BENEFITS OF AN OPERATING SYSTEM

In addition to traditional benefits like improving profits, quality, speed of delivery, and shareholder value, companies that build, implement, and sustain an operating system create a number of unique benefits that they can position as strategic advantages.

### 1. Create Predictability and Stability

The Toyota Production System, the world's most benchmarked operating system, has consistently outperformed its competitors in both total earnings and stability of earnings. Why? Because Toyota creates predictable and stable behaviors and results. When a company creates alignment around the framework it uses to run and improve the business, employees begin responding to issues and initiatives in uniform fashion. As a simple example from the Toyota system, when a line operator experiences a problem, he or she pulls a cord running along the production line to signal for help. Immediately, the supervisor (and only the supervisor) comes to the aid of the line operator to help diagnose and solve the problem, and to provide coaching as needed. This procedure repeats itself thousands of times daily at Toyota plants around the world. In comparison, most companies struggle to form a common definition of a "problem," let alone a prescribed solution. Since many problems never emerge, the company never addresses them. This leads to instability.

## 2. Reduce Time and Resources by Creating the "How-to"

GE's operating system takes employees and leaders away from crafting new practices and toward executing strategy and tactics. Businesses in all industries face an increasingly complex set of management initiatives. GE's system prescribes how to launch, resource, track, and adjust initiatives. Whether it is a new product or a six sigma project, employees do not get bogged down with discussions about the best approaches for each new initiative. Their time and energy is freed to focus on execution and implementation.

## 3. Enable Coordinated Action

Everyday, millions of Americans climb into their cars and drive to work. With few exceptions, their commutes are predictable and safe. How is it possible that millions of drivers who have never met each other function with such incredible coordination? They follow a well-defined and well-understood system to drive safely and efficiently. Imagine the chaos and danger if every driver decided which side of the road to use, how fast to travel, when to stop, and when to yield. Having high agreement on getting to destinations safely and quickly is not enough. But that describes the chaos and confusion many employees experience in their daily work routines. An operating system provides the "rules of the road" for an organization. It creates an environment wherein multiple departments and functions can coordinate action.

## 4. Provide a Teachable and Constant Approach

Employees are a company's most important and underutilized assets. But what happens when new employees arrive for their first day of work? How do they learn about the culture, the work systems, the methods and tools, and the approaches for evaluating their work? Most organizations conduct brief orientation sessions, but the real learning takes place through informal and unpredictable interactions with coworkers. In one company it was not unusual to hire new engineers, give them 10 minutes of "HR orientation" on topics such as safety and telephone use, and then send them to their supervisors, where they really learned how things were supposed to work. A company has no control over the quality and consistency of learning in informal situations. With an operating system, however, teaching is a coordinated, focused task. Employees learn their role in the system through an explicit framework. Because an operating system provides a teachable path, organizations see constancy of purpose and approach. In a sense, the operating system becomes the owner's manual of a company.

Unlike most companies, leaders at Harley-Davidson succeed their predecessors without losing momentum or direction in the organization. The company's consistent operating system allows leaders to build on the success of previous leaders instead of starting over with grand new schemes. This applies to the highest levels of the organization as evidenced by the successful handoff of CEOs from Vaughn Beals to Rich Teerlink to Jeff Bleustein to Jim Ziemer.

Contrarily, at a major automotive supplier it was not unusual to change plant managers every one to two years. By rule, the new plant manager had to come from outside the plant. In fact, the person had to come from outside the division. The rule was intended to allow people to develop and grow, but its only real effect was to constantly disrupt the direction of the organization. The employees had figured out the path of least resistance—wait out each new initiative that came with each new plant manager until he or she rotated elsewhere. There was certainly no momentum in that organization.

## 5. Offer Scalability and Portability

Operating systems provide organizations with tremendous advantages during mergers and consolidations. The purchasing company can export the system to the acquired company's operations and realize cost savings and synergies. An operating system can serve as a rare constant during the tumultuous upheaval of a merger. Wall Street gave ALCOA high marks during its acquisition of Reynolds due in large part to ALCOA's business system. The system provided a proven and predictable approach, which reaped considerable cost savings from Reynold's operations. ALCOA's business system is cited as a primary reason for the merger's success.

Operating systems also offer organizations a powerful approach during times of growth. A company can efficiently start new operations, plants, and office centers by easily connecting them with the larger enterprise. Toyota, as an example, smoothly and successfully opens new operations regularly around the world utilizing its Toyota Production System. There is little difference among the operations of the new and existing plants. The system's portability can expand even into new lines of business, or mergers and acquisitions. When a company with a strong operating system such as Danaher buys a new company, the operating system comes with it. Danaher's system is so strong, a lone representative can go into the acquired organization and transform it.

## THE OPERATING SYSTEM FRAMEWORK

How does an organization create an effective operating system? It defines the four domains of the framework: thinking, systems, tools, and evaluation.

All four domains of the operating system must work together. Once established, an operating system will seem almost transparent, as employees will use the thinking, systems, tools, and evaluation mechanisms as a matter of routine.

### Dimension One: Thinking

The thinking domain is deliberately at the center of any successful operating system (see Figure 5-1). It is the domain through which employees perceive and interpret the organization.

It provides the means to create alignment and ultimately influence culture. Thinking should incorporate a company's vision, principles, and mental models. These elements then form a lens through which employees observe everyday work to see gaps between the current and ideal states. Based on these filters, employees collect information, make decisions, and take actions. The way an organization's people think determines the quality and consistency of their actions.

How do an organization's leaders go about defining what the company should be, the values it should hold, and the mental models everyone needs as filters? First, they must be explicit about the beliefs that employees should hold when making decisions, processing information, and solving problems in everyday activities. They need to define the principles that they expect everyone to apply. Secondly, they must make the statements about vision and principles actionable. For example, stating a principle of "customer service" alone leaves too much to interpretation. Stated as, "serve customers through an intense focus on delivery time" provides employees with clearer guidance. Third, leadership must display behaviors consistent with the organization's thinking, or risk undermining credibility. A leader's behavior truly tests the validity of an organization's espoused statements.

## Thinking by Itself is Not Enough

Some organizations focus solely on the thinking domain. For example, some rely exclusively on catch-phrases and slogans to change the way employees think. Banners, placards, and videos extolling the virtues of safety, quality, and waste elimination are fine, but a company needs to back them up with capable systems and coordinated action behind the scenes. Otherwise, the disconnect often leads to a cynical and sarcastic workforce.

## Dimension Two: Systems

The systems domain defines how an organization manages and executes its routine business functions and connects the people within the organization. Systems included in this domain perform functions like material management, decision making, financial and accounting practices, human resources (HR), and work management procedures. Sometimes automation enables the systems, but automated processes are not the only part of the systems domain. Processes like leadership development, product development, performance appraisals, and governance also fall under the purview of the systems domain.

Regardless of their intentions or skill levels, employees working with flawed systems will fail. Bad systems always beat good people. As they put out the fire of the day, employees working with ineffective systems become frustrated and discouraged. To avoid ineffective systems, a company needs to consider:

- Are the systems capable of delivering the intended results?
- Do they provide the right information to the right people at the right time to appropriately manage the business?
- Are the systems robust enough to handle the complexity of situations that an organization faces?
- Are the systems free of waste?

## Systems Alone are Not Enough

The process-reengineering fad of the 1990s created companies that toyed in the systems domain. When organizations focus solely on the systems domain, they tend to want to redesign large systems and processes through process redesign, automation, and information systems as a way to cut costs and improve quality. In some cases, these efforts can and do translate to short-term improvements. But in most cases, they do not establish an infrastructure of new mental models, improvement tools, or evaluation mechanisms to sustain and continually improve. The result is organizations see step-function performance improvements that degrade over time.

## Dimension Three: Tools

While the systems domain provides the playbook to run and manage the business, the tools domain defines how to operate and improve the systems. The tools domain includes methods such as policy deployment, balanced scorecards, problem-solving techniques, kaizen practices, and six sigma.

There are many tools that a company can adopt and integrate into operations. The key is to select the right tool kit for the operating system and then make it effective and consistent (more on consistency later). It is equally important to decide which tools to avoid. Many companies have made the mistake of trying to incorporate too many tools. This often creates confusion, rather than improvement.

## Tools by Themselves are Not Enough

Most large-scale continuous improvement approaches begin and end in the tools domain; this commonly leads to failure. For years, the U.S. automotive industry attempted to import the Toyota Production System by cherry picking perceived high-impact approaches, such as the andon system, which enables a production operator to signal for immediate assistance when a problem is encountered. A number of plants incorporated the andon system and saw their overall performances actually decline. Why? In Toyota's system, many other tools such as small work teams, visual management techniques, standard work instructions, and problem-solving mechanisms support andon. Furthermore, the principle of quickly acknowledging problems, which is embedded in Toyota's culture, may not necessarily translate easily to other companies.

Importing tools into a legacy system almost always fails to drive any significant changes, because companies do not make the context for adopting them clear, and the tools themselves do not fit within the organization's broader set of principles, practices, and methods. The same way the human body rejects donated organs, organizations often reject appended methods. In both cases, there needs to be compatibility.

## Dimension Four: Evaluation

How does a company know where it stands? The final piece to building a great operating system is to define and develop evaluation mechanisms. Through the evaluation domain, an organization is able to assess where it is and where it is going. By arranging closed-loop feedback within the system, evaluation methods enable a company to determine whether the entire system is producing the desired results. As Vince Lombardi once said, "If we are not keeping score, then we are just practicing."

Evaluation systems are more than simple measurement systems, balanced or otherwise. Any approach used to diagnose and understand the current state falls in the evaluation domain. Under this definition, practices like cultural assessments, process maps, and employee engagement surveys would be considered important evaluation mechanisms.

## Evaluation Mechanisms Alone are Not Enough

Some companies confuse evaluation mechanisms with a comprehensive operating system. Their executives believe (wrongly) that measurement is the beginning, end, and middle of good management. Techniques such as balanced scorecards establish targets and encourage performance to meet those targets. The phrase, "Show me how I am measured and I will show you how I behave," becomes a reality, and often leads to the wrong behaviors since nobody is following a roadmap. In the best case, departments are able to achieve their goals and deliver some improvement to the overall system. However, companies are filled with interconnections and interdependencies. The assumption that improving all of the parts equates to improving the whole is flawed, because departments often end up working at cross purposes. Evaluation systems help companies know how they are doing. But, without the roadmap, the route can be chaotic.

## Dimension Five: Consistency

Consistency is the crucial ingredient to an operating system's effectiveness (see Figure 5-2). The other four elements (thinking, systems, tools, and evaluation) may be great independently, but without consistency, collectively they may fail. *Consistency* refers to how well each component of the operating system

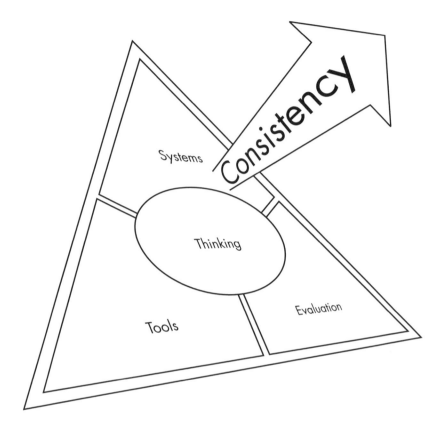

*Figure 5-2. Without consistency, the other dimensions of the operating system framework may fail.*

complements and supports the other components. If people do not have tools that are in harmony, they will not use them effectively. And if the methods of evaluation are not aligned with an operating system and its processes, organizations make bad decisions.

Consider the lean principle of "directly observe work as activities, connections, and flows." This principle should be part of the center of a lean operating system. To maintain consistency in an operating system, this principle dictates the choice and use of tools, systems, and evaluation. As examples, to help people directly observe work, a company needs tools such as value stream mapping or 3-flows diagrams. They also need to design systems, such as kanban, to help them observe. The status of kanban cards, blockages, and starves does much more than simply reduce inventory. It helps workers spot, or observe, problems as they occur so they can intervene and fix them. Evaluations and measurements also must be consistent. If only a process' output was measured, this would not be consistent with the principle of directly observing work. Instead, an organization must evaluate the process that created the result. As an example, instead of measuring the output of "on-time delivery," a company should measure the contributing processes, such as "lead time." This is one slice of a lean operating system, but it demonstrates the importance of consistency. Without consistency, an operating system can actually work against the organization.

Using the example, direct observation works with process mapping, visible systems, and in-process metrics. Because the elements are consistent, they work for, not against, each other. To gage an operating system's consistency, begin by listing all of the organization's beliefs, tools, processes, and metrics. With this list in hand, it may appear that there is, indeed, a working operating system. But inconsistent elements could be creating confusion and breakdowns in how the organization handles its daily work.

## BUILDING THE OPERATING SYSTEM FRAMEWORK

All organizations have some semblance of an operating system. At some level, work gets done. Whether the work is effective, well-designed, and well-understood by everyone is another matter. To start moving toward the ideal state, an organization first needs to make a commitment to build a framework detailing how its business should operate. For simplicity and understanding, the framework typically takes the form of a one-page document.

Companies with strong operating systems have developed them organically, over long periods of time, and often without a tacit understanding of what they were building. Though the process may seem intimidating, drafting the ideal state framework is not that difficult. Creating meaning and understanding around the framework for everyone in the organization, however—*that* is the real challenge and where the real power lies. Here are some ways to address the challenge.

1. Gather knowledge. This first step is used as a springboard to identify the thinking, systems, tools, and evaluation mechanisms that should drive the business. To begin, an inventory should be taken of what the company has and what it needs. The practice, methods, and mental models currently at play in the organization should be assessed. Look everywhere—usually best practices are found at the margins of an organization. An understanding is developed of what is and is not positively serving the organization.

   To maintain momentum with approaches and techniques that employees already understand and effectively use, it is important to blend current practices with new practices. In studying how new products were introduced into the marketplace, Joel Barker created what became known as the "Tactics of Innovation" (Barker 1998). Two of Barker's tactics are especially appropriate to introduce lean: clear message and compatible fit. "Clear message" means a company must craft the what, why, and how of its transformation message within a context that its employees can grasp. To accomplish this, a company's leaders must have a clear understanding of the current state of the business conditions, culture, and beliefs in the organization. "Compatible fit" means the company's proposed operating system must be compatible with the successful components of its current system. To promote change, a company needs to make some modifications, however.

   Benchmarking is one method used to gather knowledge. This common practice can be used to an advantage, but there is a forewarning: Over-reliance on benchmarking will mean the company will never be better than second best, because it is only following others. A company's leaders must add their own thinking to take the lead position.

A grassroots lean effort at one organization led to the development of an in-house shorthand language. The effort gained momentum, and leadership offered executive sponsorship and formal support. One of the first things to go, however, was the company's special lean language. The new "official" words may have been better, but the lack of compatible fit meant that most of those already engaged in lean rejected the new efforts, and the organization's lean transformation stalled.

2. Converge thinking. The key players are pulled together to start developing a playbook. To build the framework, a structured, facilitated process is used. The goal is to reach consensus on the framework's content and structure. Senior leadership must drive this effort. Based on experience, the conversations that occur during the process are far more significant than the actual document itself.

3. Test and modify. The new framework is tested for breadth, accuracy, and inclusiveness. To solicit input, the framework could be reviewed with all senior leaders, either individually or in focus groups. Or, focus groups of employees at all levels could be conducted. This has the added benefit of familiarizing the employee population with the effort. A full-scale organizational assessment can also help determine whether the framework lacks any current activities or details to provide sufficient robustness. An organization may spend three to four months testing, modifying, and refining its initial framework.

4. Develop expertise and infrastructure. Creating and refining the framework in and of itself generates little in the way of action within the organization. To start deploying the operating system's methods, the necessary support infrastructure needs to be built. Many organizations

form a support department to facilitate the training, communication, application, and organizational change aspects of the rollout. The team of in-house experts collaborates with senior leaders to create an overall implementation plan. An expert network could be created alongside a strong internal support team. To build an outstanding network throughout the company, action-based training on operating system practices must be provided for top individuals and leaders within the line functions. The unofficial leaders of the organization should not be forgotten—those without formal leadership roles but who wield tremendous influence.

5. Communicate and deploy. An operating system is not "real" until employees actually start doing something. A well-conceived deployment process includes administering training throughout the company, managing significant operational projects through operating system practices, establishing application areas within key business units, and beginning to roll common tools and evaluation systems out to create a sense of connection and coordination. Information is any organization's central nervous system, so an expertly crafted communication plan is vital. Employees should know the meaning and purpose of the operating system, the implementation approach, the behaviors and actions expected of them and, finally, the results of the effort—no matter how small in the beginning.

## A TALE OF TWO OPERATING SYSTEMS

To demonstrate how important the framework is to the sustainability of improvement efforts, two stories of operating system efforts are contrasted here. The authors of this book have had a great deal of experience with the development and execution of many operating systems, perhaps more than anyone. There are many dos, and even more don'ts.

## Chrysler Corporation

In the early 1990s, as Chrysler struggled with yet another bankruptcy episode, the automaker launched many initiatives aimed at improving the company's operations. Perhaps the most significant was the creation and deployment of the Chrysler operating system (COS), which initially focused on manufacturing, but quickly expanded into other support functions such as the supply chain and finance.

COS introduced consistency to several critical dimensions. Its backbone was four subsystems: human infrastructure, leveled and balanced schedules, value-added activities, and robust, capable, and in-control processes. Within the subsystems were key support processes and tools, such as kaizens (known as COS workshops) for value-added activities, and statistical process control (SPC) and failure mode and effects analysis (FMEA) for robust, capable and in-control processes. The automaker also introduced a range of measurements, including those with a broad focus, such as safety, quality, delivery, cost, and morale, as well as those with a more specific focus, such as employee grievances and defects.

But Chrysler did not clearly articulate the operating system's associated thinking or beliefs. The company's leaders understood the thinking, but did not disseminate it throughout the organization along with the rest of the operating system. They did not purposefully withhold the information, but assumed—wrongly—that the employees would automatically grasp the thinking as they rolled out the new operating system. The result was that the document, a single sheet of paper, became the operating system. There was limited thinking that lived beyond what was on that sheet. As long as employees could refer to the operating system document, everything seemed OK, and that is what drove behavior.

To demonstrate the disconnect, a previous belief at Chrysler was "manufacturing moves metal," which meant that given the choice, it always kept production going and fixed mistakes later. Under the new operating system, the automaker deployed an andon system that aimed to fix processes within the workstation—occasionally stopping the line—instead of waiting for inspection. This kind of behavior was in direct conflict with Chrysler's existing beliefs. When supervisors and managers encountered employees who stopped the line, their response was not only unhelpful, it was downright unfriendly. What was the result? Operators stopped using the andon process, and it failed to get off the ground.

COS transformation did eventually lead to significant progress and helped, along with product transformation, to save Chrysler. The automaker was even named the best-managed company of 1996 in North America by a major magazine. However, following its merger with Daimler, the company experienced a significant turnover in leadership. When the leaders left, the belief system they championed also left and the COS efforts ground to a halt. In failing to change the organization's thinking, the Chrysler operating system was unsustainable.

## DTE Energy

DTE Energy, a large gas and electric utility, took a different path to its lean transformation. A group of change agents, who migrated to the company from Chrysler and elsewhere, and had learned the COS lessons, introduced the concept to the company. After a period of significant learning and experimentation, the company's executive leadership developed the DTE Energy operating system. The company was a lean pioneer in the energy industry, and its lean journey began slowly and deliberately. Adapting an operating system designed for the automotive industry for the energy industry proved challenging.

Having had little experience in driving lean enterprise-wide, DTE Energy chose to start by adopting kaizen workshops as its standard continuous improvement method. The workshops gave departments a tool to achieve significant improvements and provided a learning field for the entire organization to experience the value of driving waste out. Knowing the journey would continue beyond kaizens, DTE Energy's senior leaders embarked on an aggressive learning effort including benchmarking trips (Toyota, Chrysler, GE, ALCOA, MACI, Bombardier), visits from various experts, on-site lectures, and other education.

Following a merger with MCN Energy, a large Michigan-based natural gas company, DTE Energy urgently needed to create one common, integrated framework for running and improving its business. It developed an operating council comprised of senior leaders in the major operating units to sponsor and champion the design and implementation of the DTE Energy operating system. Leveraging all that it had learned and reviewing significant feedback, the operating council designed the operating system framework. As a next step, it began building the principles, systems, tools, and evaluation mechanisms into the core business.

An internal facilitation and consulting group collaborated with the operating council to create a 24-month implementation plan. As the implementation has evolved and unfolded, the company has established a strong foundation for its operating system's continued growth. Some of the key accomplishments of this implementation include:

- DTE Energy has trained and developed a network of operating system experts to internally lead implementation and application within its business units.
- The company has adopted common tools throughout the enterprise to continue building a standard approach for improvement.
- DTE Energy has launched key demonstration projects and focused the application of the operating system on core business processes, resulting in significant cost savings.
- The communications strategy promotes sharing examples of applications across the enterprise to increase understanding, integration, and coordination.
- DTE Energy has created assessments to allow individual work teams to monitor their applications and utilization of the utility's operating system.

As with any transformation effort, DTE Energy has experienced challenges and course corrections along the way. Still, throughout the enterprise the evidence of success is demonstrated in the energy and commitment made to make the operating system a way of life. The primary question has shifted from "why?" to "how fast?" DTE Energy's operating system has provided everyone with a common engine to achieve the results—results that pile millions on top of millions. Just as significantly, DTE Energy's operating system is creating a culture where integration and coordination are the lynchpins of success. A piece of paper does not determine the behaviors—it is only a reference guide; the culture and principles determine the behaviors.

Creating and deploying an operating system, to be certain, is an evolutionary task; the steps provided here can be used as guidelines. As the experiences of Toyota, ALCOA, Danaher and DTE Energy demonstrate, it is a journey that grows and changes over time. But it is a journey worth taking. It is a journey that distinguishes great companies. Imagine the day when all employees at your organization will have the same response to a simple question like, "How does your organization operate?"

## REFERENCE

Barker, Joel. 1998. "Tactics of Innovation" video. St. Paul, MN: Star Thrower Distribution Corp.

**Five Dimensions of an Operating System**

1. Thinking

2. Systems

3. Tools

4. Evaluation

5. Consistency

# 6

# Relearning to Count:
# Five Lean Accounting Principles

Lean accounting is a topic that has received a great deal of attention lately—and for good reasons. Some of that attention is from the accounting profession itself, but far too much of it is coming from operations and product development as complaints lobbed at the accountants. Accounting can play an active role in either enabling or hampering lean efforts. Operating chiefs starting their lean journeys often ask who they should bring to training. It is recommended that they ask their CFOs or controllers, because they can help refine the measurement system and the role that measurements play in the organization. And, if they do not learn how to participate in the lean journey, they will impede progress.

Once enlightened to the power of lean, financial executives ask the next logical question: "How does this apply to my world?" Despite the current flurry of books, seminars, and claims by some that they have "the answer," the accounting community has not progressed very far along the lean accounting learning curve. In 2005, the accounting community is probably at the same point lean manufacturing was at in 1985. Conclusions have not been developed, and consensus is still far away. At this point, no one should accept anything as gospel in this field—including what you are about to read in this chapter. But this chapter will provide direction and address some challenges which, as they are conquered, will bring more value to the accounting practice and to its role in companies. Since there is a long way to go, you are encouraged to delve into and tackle lean accounting. You will be well ahead of the competition and rewarded for your efforts.

## A BRIEF HISTORY LESSON

In 1987, the groundbreaking book, *Relevance Lost*, made the case that accounting reports and data had lost their significance within companies (Johnson and Kaplan 1987). Reports and data had become so ineffective as management tools that they often led to wrong decisions. Since that time, little has changed. Accounting itself is more automated, more complex, and apparently more prone to obscene manipulation. But accounting is still woefully inadequate as a management tool. A survey by Ernst & Young and the Institute of Management Accountants reported that 98% of senior financial executives believe the cost information they receive is inaccurate, but only 20% have any plans to do anything about it. This highlights the disconnect between today's financial metrics and lean transformation and the gap between accountants and the people who must use the information they provide.

Accounting was created for the purpose of reporting to the outside world. It was not intended or designed to be used as an internal management and decision-making system, but that is how it is used today. To take a common example, consider overhead absorption and machine utilization. From an accounting standpoint, running a machine or process absorbs the overhead costs of the organization at a standard rate so that, in theory, when the month is out, the process has not only made a product but also made money to take care of the overhead for the company. That is the theory. In practice, when managers are measured on this variable, they are encouraged to run their equipment because it absorbs more overhead. As a result, the company did not actually make more money, but the numbers make it appear as if it did. In fact, this practice just encourages the waste of overproduction. It actually costs the company money, consuming resources for no productive end. And managers are rewarded for doing exactly the wrong thing.

For another example, consider direct labor. Many years ago, labor was the primary cost in manufacturing. Today the average is around 17% for U.S. manufacturing companies. Product cost is direct labor plus overhead. However, overhead is based on an allocation calculated by the percent of direct labor used. This means direct labor, from an accounting standpoint, is the only thing that matters. One company applied this to an extreme, measuring each plant on its direct labor content. One plant in that system bought a specialized piece of capital equipment (outlaying significant cash and increasing overhead) that removed six direct labor jobs. However, downtime was 30% and it took five more expensive indirect labor jobs to handle the process. The purchase was a bad decision, but another one that was rewarded through the accounting and measurement system.

Over the years, lean has helped the manufacturing world change its way of thinking and working. Taiichi Ohno, a founding father of the Toyota Production System, said that, "The Toyota Production System is not just a production system." Most companies have overlooked that point and equate lean with lean manufacturing. Before focusing on finance and accounting, it is important to note that product development, sales, and marketing are even farther back on the lean learning curve.

The notion of lean accounting is fairly new, and it is likely that the five lean accounting principles presented here will evolve as more is learned.

## LEAN ACCOUNTING PRINCIPLE ONE: ACCOUNTING IS A PROCESS, NOT JUST A PROFESSION

Certainly, well-trained accounting professionals are good for accounting departments. But accounting processes and work designs are greater indicators of success. Just like manufacturing, accounting has inputs and outputs. The better the process flow, the more efficient and effective the results.

Every operation can be measured on safety, quality, delivery, and cost. Compared to manufacturing, how many accounting departments know the performance metrics for each one of their processes? While overtime is not a cost factor for most salaried personnel, it certainly affects the physical and mental health of accounting professionals. Overtime in the accounting field has mushroomed to epidemic proportions. Some of the overtime blame can be placed on new reporting requirements and personnel shortages, but the real culprits are wasteful processes.

Most financial departments spend a vast amount of their resources on transactional processes. Similar to plant managers in companies that are not yet lean, controllers run around putting out fires created by broken processes. Instead, accounting departments should adapt lean rules, principles, and tools to make their processes more effective and efficient. Employees could use a kaizen workshop, or just go observe work and eliminate waste themselves. If it takes four weeks to close the company's books, lean could be used to condense the time to four days. If it takes four days, the department should work to reduce the time to one day. The same tools could be applied to the dreaded budgeting process, if it can even be called a process. Errors should be eliminated by error proofing and using visual management to quickly bring problems to the surface.

The point of Principle One is that an organization can not tackle processes effectively with good people and information technology alone. It must design the work—the activities, connections, and flows—to produce the desired results and continuously improve from there. By starting with this principle, an organization will gain understanding and resources to help with the subsequent four lean accounting principles.

## LEAN ACCOUNTING PRINCIPLE TWO: GO BEYOND THE NUMBERS

Principle Two is linked to the core lean principle: directly observe work as activities, connections, and flows. It is not suggested that the numbers be thrown away. Numbers have their place, but they should not be used as the primary tool for understanding the current state. Numbers provide an abstract view of reality. They are not reality itself. To seek understanding, the truest goal of accounting, a company's leaders need to dig deeper than the numbers.

Here is a brief story demonstrating the problems that can occur when organizations ignore Principle Two. A CFO was challenging his plant manager on overtime costs that were apparently running out of control. The plant manager was fighting back, claiming to need even more overtime. The CFO's numbers indicated that order sizes had increased, which compounded the frustration, since we all "know" that larger batches are cheaper than one. Frustrated, the CFO went to the plant (finally) to see what was really happening. The plant manager showed him that the order size on one part had exceeded its normal percentage within the product mix. The machine that ran the parts had a turntable so that operators could load in parts on one side while the machine worked on the other side's parts. To improve flow, different tools were often put on each side of the turntable so that it could produce a variety parts at the same time, reducing idle time for the machine. Because the volume of this particular part had increased so much, there were not enough other parts in the volume mix to rotate back and forth on the turntable. As a result, the machine sat idle while parts were exchanged on only one side of the turntable. Upon seeing this, the CFO better understood the problem (although developing a solution was still difficult). Instead of arguing numbers, the plant manager and CFO were able to concentrate on decision-making and problem-solving directed toward the real problem at hand. The lesson: you can not see with reports what you can see with your own eyes. Dwight Eisenhower had this lesson in mind when he said, "Farming looks mighty easy when your plow is a pencil and you are a thousand miles from the corn field." Whether an engineer or a CEO, observing work as it transpires yields the most reliable information.

This story plays out in companies every day. Financial and accounting departments are uniquely qualified to understand the cost drivers of the business. But they need more than numbers to appreciate the whole story.

## LEAN ACCOUNTING PRINCIPLE THREE: TRANSITION FROM COST COP TO COACH

The traditional role of the controller (and even the origin of the title) is to control people's actions so that they do not spend more money than they should for the sake of the business. The fundamental assumption is that without this personal watchdog, each individual would seek to do what is best or easiest for him or her, not necessarily for the company. The relationship is fundamentally based on mistrust, deception, and misinformation. Everyone tries to game the system. The first thing many people learned in Manufacturing 101 is how to manipulate the numbers. Instead of facing common enemies such as waste, bad processes, or poor customer service, controllers and the people at the companies with whom they work view each other as enemies. This adversarial relationship is rooted in the past. Understanding a company's numbers was once a narrowly distributed capability, since the people who worked at companies were not as educated and knowledgeable as they are today. Unlike contemporary lean organizations, almost all decision-making was highly centralized. Accounting, therefore, served few internal customers.

Given the prevailing culture and operating patterns, controllers must go beyond the role of cost cop and become true partners, advisors, and coaches to operating managers. Some examples of nontraditional roles include:

- designer/architect of operational, not just financial, measurement systems to be used by everyone from front-line employees to CEOs;
- designer, implementer, and manager of the process by which managers use data and measurement for daily assessment and decision-making; and
- coach of managers to combine direct observation of the system with an understanding of cost drivers and how to put that understanding to effective use (see Principle Two).

Measures are akin to looking in the rearview mirror: they typically tell you where you have been, not where you are going. Operational measures help a work group, whether a department or on the front line, manage its process. But they need to be predictive. For example, if a team has developed a sound safety audit, a good audit score should predict a low incidence of injuries. If the score drops, the team can predict that it will have more injuries. Most teams simply measure lost-time injuries. Since they already know about lost time, the metric does not help them manage the process. The financial organization should design operational measurement systems that are predictive, actionable, owned, and timely for line management.

The strategies discussed here will help turn a controller into an operating partner instead of an adversary. How might this transformation be encouraged? Turn financial staffs at every level into vacation replacements for line management—corporate controllers for operating VPs, plant controllers for plant managers, all the way to young financial analysts for front-line supervision. Understanding and a common language can help bridge the chasm.

## LEAN ACCOUNTING PRINCIPLE FOUR: THE FIRST FILTER IS VALUE AND THE CUSTOMER

Ultimately, customers pay your salary. So, the lens of the customer and of value should always serve as the first filter for decisions and process design. Instead, most companies *manage* the customer while they make decisions based on internal filters, assumptions, and short-term gains. Almost all long-term successful firms have a "customer-first" viewpoint. (Even those that espouse "employees first" fundamentally assume that happy employees will better serve customers.)

To adopt the lens of the customer, a company's leaders should make process and financial decisions only after asking, "What does the customer value, and how might this decision help or hurt that value?" Processes developed for the company and its internal needs are often done so at the expense of the customer. Look at your phone bill as an example. Does it look like that document is created for you as the customer? Each line item is there to match up to some internal budget. While convenient for the manager who can find his or her responsibility on the bill, the customer is left confused and frustrated.

To provide a common example of lean transformation, when a company streamlines processes, it requires less in inventory. This prompts a thorough review of what is actually on hand, and typically reveals a plethora of obsolete and unnecessary inventory. A company is faced with the dilemma of either ditching the excess inventory and writing it off or slowly trying to manage it out of the system. Financial executives almost always want to slowly siphon the inventory off so it will not affect the company's financial statement. (Note that this is the pattern in private companies as well as public.) The right thing to do for the process, the customer, and the business, however, is to immediately dispose of the waste. It ties up floor space ($), requires extra work and resources ($), and no matter how careful the company is, there is always the risk of it getting mixed with current product ($). Whether there is a failure to understand the negative impact of the decision or a failure to use the customer/value filter does not matter. The point is organizations sometimes make bad decisions based on numbers and perception alone.

Budgets offer another example. Most budget processes rely on last year's budget. Sometimes, constraints or wishes, whether internal or external, play a role. Rarely do the people crafting budgets begin with a clear image and articulation of what customers want and do not want. Rarely do they consider whether line items add value for customers. Instead of developing a budget and then working to meet it, a company should develop a budget to meet its needs, which reflects its customers' needs and provides a lens for continual improvement.

## LEAN ACCOUNTING PRINCIPLE FIVE: MAKE DATA ACCESSIBLE FOR THE CUSTOMER

"Customer" refers to the traditional customer as well as the people inside the company who make decisions and have an impact on the organization's performance. "Accessible" does not mean giving everyone a link and a password to the accounting database. It means making financial reports easier to understand, more relevant, more actionable, and timelier. It also means generating awareness and understanding to make the information available at *every* level of the organization.

The basis for all financial reports is external reporting; internal usability, therefore, is a secondary concern. Reports compile and aggregate data to offer a standardized view of the company compared to past performance and other companies. Companies need new ways to present data for their internal audiences. CFOs could, for example, rewrite income and balance sheets in plain English so that individuals at every level could understand and use them.

To help develop an effective cost understanding of the business, financial executives need to become teachers and coaches. First, they need to be students—students of lean, the profession, the business, and the industry. This will help organizations avoid what is referred to as "kaizen striping of the parking lot." This is when an organization focuses on improvement efforts that will have little impact on performance. Reports, authoritative structures, sign-offs, or rules will not cut it—teaching is a must.

## NEXT STEPS

To review, despite many years of learning and experimentation, the accounting function is still at the beginning stages of identifying true lean accounting practice and performance management. The ideas put forward here are meant to encourage everyone to push the envelope and continue to experiment. Ideas should be brought to the surface and shared freely and openly so that companies can stand on the shoulders of those who took steps before them. This is not the time to close doors and be protective. It is sometimes forgotten that lean efforts began when other companies, notably Toyota, opened their doors and shared what they learned.

CFOs are encouraged to put together an action plan (do not study too much) and get started. Progress will generate more learning and understanding and allow movement to the next step.

## REFERENCE

Johnson, Thomas H. and Kaplan, Robert S. 1987. *Relevance Lost: the Rise and Fall of Management Accounting*. Boston, MA: Harvard Business School Press.

### Five Lean Accounting Principles

1. Accounting is a process, not just a profession

2. Go beyond the numbers

3. Transition from cost cop to coach

4. The first filter is value and the customer

5. Make data accessible for the customer

# 7

## Move It or Lose It: Five Keys to Lean Material Management

Lean manufacturing has come a long way in the past two decades, moving beyond basic manufacturing into everything from healthcare to financial services. Lean made an early impact on material management, but may have missed a turn along its journey. Today, lean material handling and control, from the shop floor to the supply chain, is in need of a reexamination. To date, lean material efforts have been based on tools and their deployment. Lean, however, should be about principles, or thinking, which constantly drives progress to the ideal state. Many companies avow this in their training, but focus on tools in practice.

Traditionally, lean material management has always been an extension of lean manufacturing. Since the manufacturing folks are often the most experienced in lean, they typically help develop lean material management. However, it can be a mistake to base lean material management on lean manufacturing. Instead, companies should try taking a fresh look.

Five key concepts are presented in this chapter to help a company take a fresh look at lean transformation for material management. Using these five concepts as the basis for assessment, a company's leaders will be able to avoid typical gaps and barriers, stay on course, and make effective judgments and improvements.

## CONCEPT ONE: INFORMATION BLINDNESS

As computing power has evolved into a commodity and software providers dominate the headlines, there has been a significant push for more visibility of every nook and cranny of systems. Phrases such as "real-time" and "unit-level data" fill marketing materials and articles. The underlying theory is that if a company can get real-time information at the push of a button, it will be able to react to events faster and more effectively. The fundamental problem with this theory is its focus on reacting to events and problems. Reacting is also known as *firefighting*. And lean aims to eliminate firefighting. Its goal is to design systems that respond to a company's needs.

Consider this analogy: air traffic controllers know the speed, direction, and location of every aircraft. They constantly assess flight patterns and give planes directions. Imagine that there are traffic controllers for vehicles on highways. They would assess road conditions and react by telling drivers what to do next. They would collect the speed, location, size, and direction of every vehicle on the road, filter out what is important, and tell drivers when to speed up, brake, and turn. When controllers have two dozen planes on their radars with very clear rules and plenty of buffer space, directing air traffic is a manageable system. With thousands of cars condensed into a small area, very little buffer, and varying interpretation of the rules, directing highway traffic would quickly turn into a disaster. If the movement of material and resources in your organization were compared to this analogy, which process would it more resemble?

Most material management systems are as complex and fast-moving as the highway system. But that does not prevent the development of systems that monitor and manage material down to the second and unit. An advertisement for a highway traffic control system might state, "Make your organization respond rapidly to changing needs in the marketplace by dynamically creating an efficient and controllable supply chain." This sounds good, right? But in practice, chaos and accidents would ensue.

The current state changes too quickly to manage the system based on heaps of information.

Most material management systems are similar. Many people, companies, and machines make independent decisions. And they need more than just a lot of information to make effective decisions. Anyone can make a decision that works best in the moment, but this is not the same as making decisions consistently for the good of the system or enterprise. Going back to the traffic analogy, all the information combined is not half as vital as one critical piece of information: when does the person in front of you put on his brakes? The "more information is better" myth is alive and well, but even with a deluge of information people can still be clueless about their next step. Instead of more information, a company needs valuable information. Information needs to be sourced as close to the point of activity as possible. Systems need to be designed to give people the information they need to determine their next action—and nothing more.

Because they provide timely, focused information, many lean practices rely on card-based systems such as kanban. For many applications, low-tech solutions like kanban cards, or even a kanban square painted on the floor, work well at providing simple and direct information signals. It is not that the use of a computerized system is bad, but when it is designed to do more than is needed, it is waste.

## CONCEPT TWO: ELIMINATE THE WHITE SPACE

Every activity, whether it is handling material or information, has a beginning and an end. But there is often white space between the points where one person's activity ends and the next person's activity picks up. When someone fills out section A of a form and sends it away to have section B completed, many people may touch it in between. *This* is where much of the waste sets in. Every process in every industry, whether it is material, information, or service, has five distinct steps: queue, setup, run, wait, and move. For decades, the focus has been on the run part of the process: running the machine, building the forecast, or unloading the truck. This is where organizations direct most of their energy. While it is important and offers opportunities for adding value, run is not the most wasteful process. There is plenty of waste in the other four steps, however.

In the following example, consider that the material being moved is your family. (Of course, your family is much more important than material). You visit Walt Disney World and go to the Pirates of the Caribbean ride. What is the first thing you do? You wait in line (queue). When you get to the end of the line, you can not just hop on the boat. The ride operators have to get the other people off (setup). Then you get on and go through the ride (run). When the ride is over, you have to wait for other people to get off of the boat (wait). Finally, you pack up your family and mosey to the next ride (move). There you have it: queue, setup, run, wait, and move. Now imagine Disney wanted to improve your lead-time through the Magic Kingdom. It could make the Pirates' boat go twice as fast, which would focus on the only value-added step in the process. Similarly, many companies put all of their efforts into making processes go faster. Companies must focus on the queue, setup, wait, and move steps to drive out waste, particularly in materials management.

## CONCEPT THREE: RIGHT-SIZE EVERYTHING— RIGHT TOOL, RIGHT PLACE, RIGHT TIME, AND RIGHT COST

There is a tendency in any process to be looking for the best: the fastest equipment, the software with the most features, the biggest space. This is characterized by the adage, "He who dies with the most toys, wins!" But, if someone buys software and only uses half of its features, that is waste. The person who wanted the software might try to use more of the features, but if they do not add value, he or she is wasting the company's time. And more importantly, the person should not have bought the bloated software in the first place. Whenever the authors of this book visit a warehouse or distribution operation, we invariably hear, "We need updated software, more space, and more capable equipment." While these things may make life easier and improve expenses by 10%, they do not make the company better if they add 300% to the capital requirements. Lean is about doing more with less and about using creativity before using capital.

One company manufactured a variety of needles, but its highest volume item was syringes. The needles were manufactured at one corner of the plant, and the other end of the plant made the injection-molded housings. The company used automated assembly equipment, but located it near the needle manufacturing process. A massive amount of waste was generated in getting the injection-molded housings, which were light but bulky, to assembly, including boxing, packing, moving, unpacking, and waiting for a hi-lo for transportation. Brainstorming a solution, the team first discussed moving the injection molding process next to the machining process. This solution would not have eliminated a lot of the problems and would have cost a great amount. Next, the team thought about installing elevators and overhead conveyors. This solution was cheaper, but did not get rid of most of the waste either. Inspired by a lunch break errand, the team used creativity before capital. One of the team members went to the bank to deposit his paycheck using a remote drive-up window. A pneumatic vacuum tube whisked his check into the bank. Inspired, he and the team designed a system to vacuum up the light plastic housings and dump them directly into the assembly equipment. The total cost was $3,100.

In many situations, people tend to start with the solution and then go looking for a problem. Instead, start with the problem—the pain—and when its root cause is fully understood, create the solution. Things should not be purchased to create another workaround. Buy things that actually solve the problem.

## CONCEPT FOUR: MOVING ONE INCH IS STILL A TRANSPORT

For a long time, the telecommunications industry created tremendous bandwidth only to be stymied by one nagging link, called "the last mile." This bottleneck caused overcapacity because customers could not get data in or out of the vast network. While the telecommunications industry has since resolved the problem, material management has a similar dilemma. Organizations have designed elegant and massive solutions to better move material and information across time zones, miles, and companies. Entire industries have spawned to tackle the problems. But once the container or the information arrives at its destination, there is often chaos with many people at the receiving end moving and dispatching items. Perhaps they turn the enterprise requirements planning (ERP) system outputs into handwritten notes. While tools such as radio frequency identification (RFID), handheld readout devices, and other solutions are chipping away at the problem, it still needs years of work.

Lean tools can come to the rescue with concepts such as auto-unload. Loading a machine of any kind requires articulation, manipulation, and precision—all very expensive for automation. Unloading requires one thing: transport. Auto-unload marshals the most efficient energy source available: gravity. Best of all, it is free. The application simply requires a little ingenuity and engineering for each specific location.

For example, a work cell without auto-unload might involve picking up a part from machine A, putting it down next to machine B, unloading machine B, putting that part down next to machine B, picking up the first part, loading machine B, picking up the other finished part, and taking it to machine C. Whew! Using auto-unload, the process might involve picking up a part from machine A, moving and loading it into machine B, picking up the part from the auto-unload tray, and moving it to machine C. With often little more than a kick-lever, a chute, and a tray, companies can forego incredible waste. Where in your operation do you consume vast resources to move material or information an inch?

## CONCEPT FIVE: ELIMINATE FUNCTIONAL TUNNEL VISION

Current reality is not always what it seems. Members of a plant management team were once asked to describe what lean meant to them. The quality manager cited error-proofing and first-time-through capability, and the industrial engineering (IE) manager said it was efficient job layout and standard work instructions. The maintenance manager mentioned total productive maintenance (TPM), while the controller focused on cost reduction. The materials manager also had a narrow focus when he replied, "It's about pulling material and reduction of inventory." There was no argument with any of these answers, since they were not wrong. But they were all incomplete.

While everyone has a role to play, people should not approach their roles with a partial view of current reality and an incomplete view of what the organization needs to achieve. People need to eliminate their tunnel vision. The focus should not be on good material management solutions. It should be on the contributions material management can make toward the development of an effective and complete lean system that serves the customers with what they need, when they need it, and without waste. Is this issue the same for all functions, the ones mentioned above along with finance, sales and marketing, and product development? Yes, but it takes on greater importance with material management because, as a whole, it is often the hub of information through which the rest of the organization is connected. Material management needs to approach lean transformation more holistically. Those in material management can often take the lead in driving an organization toward a common and integral view of their own re-creation.

## CONCLUSION

Material management has been on board with lean concepts for possibly as long as any other function in organizations. Most of the lean solutions that have been used for years still work. Instead of replacing these tried and true solutions, the focus should be on supplementing them. Currently, many material management professionals are automating the solutions they had already been using, making them more efficient and sometimes more effective. This part of the organization has become a cost center, consuming significant investment dollars for new systems and system upgrades. Of course every project is written with a positive return on investment (ROI), but there are many more dollars available. A few organizations need to resume driving toward the ideal state to break through the current boundaries. The five concepts outlined in this chapter can provide some guidance. Those who break through to the next level will pull the entire material management practice with them.

### Five Keys to Lean Material Management

1. Information blindness

2. Eliminate the white space

3. Right-size everything—right tool, right place, right time, and right cost

4. Moving one inch is still a transport

5. Eliminate functional tunnel vision

8

# Service on a Silver Platter:
# Five Factors for Lean Service

Traditionally, most people associate lean with manufacturing and related enterprises. To be clear, "lean manufacturing" has no place in service organizations; lean manufacturing belongs in manufacturing organizations. But lean's definition and application is broader. Lean was never meant to be the exclusive province of manufacturing, but that is the perception—and therefore the reality. Service industries mostly ignore lean's tremendous transformation potential. However, with some tweaking of the tools, lean principles and concepts apply equally well in service settings.

Admittedly, applying lean in a service environment is just plain harder. Service processes, which are cross-functional by their very nature, can be difficult to see, and documentation and measurement are sparse. However, the results can be astounding. To get a sense of the potential, here is a simple value-added test. A *value-added activity* is defined by three strict criteria:

1. The activity must be valued by the customer who is willing to pay for it.

2. It must change the product or service.

3. The activity must be done right the first time.

Stand in the middle of a manufacturing operation—any manufacturing operation—take a mental snapshot of the process, and determine what percentage of people are performing value-added work. Repeat the same evaluation in a service organization. You will inevitably find a smaller percentage of people in a service organization adding value for their customers. How, then, can lean help in a service environment? This chapter will explore what a lean service organization looks like, what challenges it might face as it embarks on lean transformation, and how it can get started on its lean journey.

## WHAT ARE THE OPERATIONAL OBJECTIVES?

Many service organizations do not have clear operational objectives. Of course, service and revenue are always considerations, but they are not operational objectives. They are only results—autopsies of the process. Employees in service organizations lack guidance on *how* their organization should operate. Lean manufacturing complements result metrics with operational metrics such as lead time, first-time-through capability, and inventory turns. Likewise, service organizations need to create operational metrics that are predictive, help guide action, and provide focus.

Some manufacturing metrics may still apply in a service environment, but collecting data, such as first-time-through capability and lead time, may prove more difficult. Other metrics are unique to service organizations, including the percentage rate of customer needs served in the first attempt and the percentage of value-added time per service worker. Because a service organization does not typically have a clear a picture of its current reality, predictive operational metrics help describe its true performance.

## HOW IS LEAN SERVICE DIFFERENT FROM MANUFACTURING?

Compared to manufacturing, some service-related problems are more pronounced, while others are subtler. Creating change in a service environment, however, involves the most significant differences.

In most service organizations that have been visited by the authors of this book, someone with lean experience who is charged with taking us on a tour inevitably leads us to the supply area, the back office, or a part of the operation that most closely resembles manufacturing. This underscores the narrow perception of lean and demonstrates that it is often looked for in the wrong places. Lean thinking should help people look for improvement opportunities where conventional wisdom fails them.

## FIVE FACTORS FOR LEAN SERVICE

The following five factors focus on how lean in service organizations is distinct from lean in manufacturing or operational environments. The waste is hiding. Service organizations need to solve the small stuff. Although it is harder to see the process, service organizations need to design around and for the customer, and organizing events is necessary to find the waste.

### Factor One: Waste is Hiding

To help highlight service problems, an organization can view them through the lens of the seven wastes: overproduction, waiting, motion, transportation, overprocessing, inventory, and defects. The seven wastes also offer a language by which a lean organization can discuss service challenges.

Lean organizations are committed to the constant elimination of waste—by everybody. Manufacturing organizations often focus on inventory, especially early in their lean journeys, because it ties up lots of cash. In service organizations (except retail and distribution), however, inventory is a minor factor. More prominent waste factors include waiting, motion, overprocessing, and service.

For example, hospital nurses typically seek the best quality footwear, because they travel many miles each day (waste of motion). Studies have shown that nurses can spend two-thirds of their time looking for information or material, dubbed "nursing the system," thereby leaving little time for nursing the patient, the true value-added work. The Pittsburgh Regional Healthcare Initiative's goal is to bring a variant of lean called Perfecting Patient Care™ (PPC), to its healthcare members. In collaboration with that organization, the authors of this book visited a hospital that was celebrating a small success (of many successes) as part of its PPC journey. Previously, nurses had to seek out a supervisor anytime they needed to unlock the medicine. This problem often tied up enough time that it accounted for one full-time employee. By applying the PPC perspective, the facility determined that there was not any reason why all nurses could not have keys. Today, nurses are able to apply the saved time to caring for their patients.

During a lean class at the Pittsburgh hospital, plenty of waiting waste was observed. Ninety minutes were spent observing the physical therapy (PT) and occupational therapy (OT) departments. Most days patients visited both areas. Since OT was near the patients' rooms, escorts always placed patients there first. Once OT was completely full, escorts began directing patients to PT. By that time, OT was releasing patients and sending them to PT, creating a huge line. This uneven ebb and flow of patients created an average wait of 15 minutes; some waited as long as 45 minutes. It was determined that by using a visual management system to ensure an even distribution of patients across OT and PT, the hospital could easily cut the wait time by 75%.

Jamie Flinchbaugh recently visited a different hospital with his wife for the delivery of his son. He tracked the average wait times for patient requests and calculated that it was over 30 minutes. Tellingly, the shortest wait times were for relatively trivial issues, while urgent issues took the longest. Some requests were never fulfilled. (By the way, there is really no such thing as waiting waste for the actual delivery of babies; it is all value added.)

Overprocessing waste can sometimes be hard to detect, because it is often disguised as "we are doing more for the customer." But processes that exceed what customers value, yet offer no benefits are, indeed, waste. In a manufacturing environment, people can readily discover and eliminate overprocessed features. In a service setting, however, overprocessing examples are subtler and can seem insignificant; but small improvements can add up to major savings. For example, even when guests are staying more than one night, hotels often replace the soap and shampoo in guest rooms after one use. Usually, guests would have no problem reusing their own soap twice. Consider the fast food chain that stuffs 20 napkins in a bag for one person (unless you really *need* 20 napkins, as some of us do). Or how about a new car dealership where a service technician writes down customer and vehicle information on a sheet of paper, only to walk a few feet to a computer where he keys in the same information? While they may seem minor, when events like these occur across hundreds of thousands of customers, in thousands of different ways, the cumulative toll can be astounding.

Defect waste is obviously bad. In service settings, it can be particularly dangerous. Service errors are about five times more likely to lose customers than product failures. Building a better mousetrap is not enough; you also have to deliver and service it in an efficient and effective manner.

## Factor Two: Sweat the Small Stuff

In a lean manufacturing environment, a combination of new skills and a system designed to make problems visible enables daily problem solving. In a pull process, when two operations are connected through stock replenishment signals, a problem at either end of the customer-supplier chain immediately surfaces. This is an often misunderstood aspect of what pull is about; but bringing problems to the surface, not reducing inventory, is one of a pull system's primary purposes. As problems rise to the surface on a daily basis, an organization can solve them, thereby making its systems stronger one problem at a time.

In a service organization, problems are less visible. That is because the buffer, the thing that shields the organization from little problems, is not a tangible element, such as inventory, but something more elusive: time. Instead of working around problems, a service organization must make them visible and create structures to force workers to solve problems as they occur.

One natural gas supply organization has service stations that handle a variety of tasks including leak repairs, installations, and appliance maintenance. To avoid being overwhelmed, it focused lean on one issue that would have a positive ripple effect and would involve and affect its front-line workers: ensuring that technicians get to their first customers by 8:30 a.m. When a technician failed to meet the objective, he and the supervisor would engage in problem solving. Most problems were minor, but the constant problem solving helped the organization reach its goal. In fact, the percentage of technicians reaching the first customer by 8:30 a.m. rose from a paltry 11% to a world-class 93%. Modifications included dedicated locations where staff could leave needed parts and information, coordinated visual layouts for truck parking and keys, and a structured help chain for technicians to get the right assistance when they needed it and without repercussions. With a 93% on-time record, workdays have been more consistent and predictable—allowing even more room and resources for further improvements. Barriers still get in the way, but in the spirit of continuous improvement, the technicians continue to engage in problem solving.

The company continues to solve many problems by adopting simple, alternative methods that are consistent with its objectives. For example, the off-shift tested parts so that they were all approved before the day shift arrived for work. Also, the company reorganized call assignments so that, when possible, the first call was no more than 15 minutes from the station and subsequent calls were no more than 15 minutes from each previous location.

## Factor Three: It is Hard to See the Process

Direct observation of work is one of the most challenging lean skills to master. Practitioners must be able to observe a process and truly understand how the activities, connections, and flows of the process are linked to the results. A manufacturing environment lends itself to the practice and development of direct observation. The process comes alive like a ballet with the motion of people, equipment, and material. But it is much harder to observe processes for service tasks, such as accounts payable, requisition fulfillment, or evaluations. Tools such as process mapping can help develop observation skills. However, in service organizations, what people do and the product, information, or service are often on different tracks. Instead of leading to a better process, putting two distinct processes on the same map only causes confusion. Separate maps can be used to explore different aspects of the process. An *activity map* captures people's actions. A *product/process map* captures what happens to a product or service. As an organization captures current reality, it needs to look at how it designs and executes activities, connections, and process flows.

An automotive dealership is another kind of service-oriented business. One dealership engaged in counter-productive processes and had a "silo" mentality between departments. By observing work, it was found that parts availability was preventing the service technicians from finishing their work within prescribed times. This was a process problem: the people requesting parts and those filling the orders used different terms to identify the parts. Also, to request parts, technicians had to walk over to the service window, wait in line, and ask for the parts they needed. The connection was broken. To solve the problem, a system was set up whereby technicians key in their parts requests at a terminal in the service bay. When the items are ready for pick up (at a designated drop location) the parts department notifies the technician. While technicians still have to wait for parts, the wait time has decreased—and they are able to spend the wait time working on value-added tasks in the service bay rather than waiting in line.

## Factor Four: Design Around and for the Customer

Lean organizations focus on providing value for the customer. In a manufacturing environment, the process does not directly touch the customer; it creates the products that touch the customer. In service organizations, however, value and process are often one and the same. The customer is typically the beginning, middle, and end of the process.

From the customers' perspective, value should be more than a design activity. It should be an everyday lens. A service defect is a major customer problem. But a service organization can not just inspect the end results of its processes. Because the customer is so close, every employee action is a chance to either provide or destroy value. Starbucks provides more value than a cup of hot coffee. Each store provides a comfortable, convenient, and reliable environment. And they can charge for the extra value. Not all coffee drinkers value or are willing to pay for the Starbucks experience, so they go somewhere else. Whatever the service, it is important to deeply understand how different types of customers have different needs. By understanding these different audiences, a business can customize its processes and services to offer the right kinds and amounts of value to each subgroup.

To design around the customer and give them what they want, an organization needs to consider what impact its processes have on customers. How much of customers' time does an organization waste by making them wait for service or rework? How many times does an organization ask its customers to provide the same information over and over? For example one major airline asks all of its qualified passengers that check in on-line or at a kiosk whether they would like to upgrade to First Class—*before* the reservations system checks to see if First Class seating is available or even an option. Each request only takes about 15 seconds; but each 15-second delay is a painful reminder that this airline does not value its customers' time.

Blockbuster recently launched a campaign to change the way it interacts with its customers. It is not providing a new product or service—it is still renting movies for a fee. But the company looked at how much time its customers spent driving to its stores, browsing the shelves, waiting in line to pay, and driving home. (And, it undoubtedly looked at the meteoric rise of Netflix and others.) With Blockbuster's new mail-in service, the company has eliminated a lot of the burden for those customers who are interested in the service. And, unlike Netflix, when customers want their movies *now*, they still can go to the brick and mortar Blockbuster store.

For an organization offering products and services that are considered necessities, it is not as critical to infuse them with value. But an organization that provides necessities needs to pay particular attention to how it consumes its customers' money—and especially their time. Time is the currency of the 21st century. In designing around customers, it should be considered that, to a degree, time often has greater value than money. A person can always get more money, but lost time is gone forever. The moral: do not waste customers' time.

## Factor Five: Events are Necessary

Lean is *not* about events, it is about everyday behaviors, skills, and thinking. But events help create the right environment and deliver results. There is often substantial resistance to change in service organizations. Events such as kaizen workshops can break through cultural barriers and help nudge change along.

It is usually difficult to deploy lean practices and skills in service settings. One obstacle is that customers are often part of the process. Stopping a process in its tracks to apply lean with customers can be difficult. But, events can make it easier by pulling people off the front line and placing them into the transformation process where they can be invisible to customers. For example, a customer should not be told by order fulfillment to wait an extra week for shipment while improvements are being made. Similarly, a restaurant does not expect to drag its patrons into the kitchen to participate in its redesign.

When customers can be involved in the improvements, there is a lot to gain. Not only will an organization's processes be improved, but the customers' experience can be improved as well. Working side-by-side in the war against waste can help an organization build camaraderie with its customers. The downside is that the organization could risk exposing too much of its inner workings and dirty laundry; if customers do not like what they see, they may not wait for improvements. An organization needs to balance both sides of the equation to see what works best.

A word of caution: while events are necessary, an organization should not over-rely on them. Otherwise, events may become the only mechanism for change, which severely limits an organization's potential for performance improvement.

Some early events should focus on creating a living lean model. In a retail company, a single storefront may serve as the lean model. In an office setting, it might be one element or flow through the organization. To help explain lean and get employees on the lean bandwagon, living models are far more effective than theories, words, or training alone. By focusing on a small area or department of five to 20 people, an organization can quickly create a living example of what lean could look like across the enterprise—and thereby accelerate the journey for the entire organization. Living models also serve as laboratories to test applications, experiment with implementation options, and help anticipate issues the organization will face when it undertakes a broader transformation.

## CASE STUDIES

In a manufacturing environment, lean often focuses on efficiency. In a service setting, however, quality and delivery of service are the highest priority. Making lean work in a service organization poses a greater challenge, but it is a great opportunity for a company to distinguish itself from its competition. Lean takes hard work, but it can quickly—and continually—yield impressive results. Consider the results of the following two case studies.

### REACH Air Ambulance

In the air ambulance business, every minute counts. In the course of over 10,000 helicopter transports and 3,500 fixed-wing (airplane) transports, REACH Air Medical Services, located in Northern California since 1987, has developed a great reputation for rapid response. With an emphasis on pediatric critical care, REACH serves about 3,000 patients a year. Its hospital-to-hospital transports represent 60% of the business, and the remaining 40% is 911-call responses. Working closely with several large receiving hospitals and approximately 200 sending hospitals, the company operates five, fully staffed, round-the-clock helicopter operation bases, and one fixed wing base. Onboard each helicopter is a flight nurse and a flight paramedic. The airplanes include a flight nurse and a respiratory therapist.

REACH began its lean transformation in 2002. As with many companies who equate lean with manufacturing, its leaders were initially skeptical of lean's benefits. Today however, Jennifer Hardcastle, REACH's director of program development, is a lean believer. "After attending the lean class where I was exposed to the foundation of lean rules and principles, I realized how lean thinking could significantly improve our response time and the critical time spent at a patient's bedside preparing for hospital transport." She continues, "Implementing tools like value stream mapping back at our facility helped us to realize how many broken links there were along the chain between REACH and our hospital customers—and how structuring a better flow path could help us deliver faster and better patient care."

Before REACH embarked on its lean journey, it had no process in place for hospitals to indicate the urgency of patients' air ambulance needs. Using lean rules such as structure every activity, clearly connect every customer/supplier, and simplify every flow, REACH improved the situation dramatically. First, it studied the process flow between hospitals and REACH, and developed internal and hospital site teams. Hardcastle explains, "We worked together to come up with standards to define our acute Level One patients—those requiring the most urgent care. We identified what staff members could expect when they encounter patients and the processes involved in emergency treatment. For this level of patient, two, three, or four minutes can mean the difference between life and death, so process efficiency through lean thinking took on the highest level of importance."

Using the teams' new process flow, a facility can call REACH's dispatch center and indicate that it has an urgent Level One request. The air ambulance company sends an aircraft to the outgoing facility (point A) even if a destination site (point B) is not yet known. Previously, REACH did not send an aircraft until point B was determined. Critical time was often wasted making phone calls and arrangements. Now, 90% of the time REACH confirms point-B arrangements by the time its ambulances arrive for patient pickup. The new process can eliminate up to 40 minutes of waiting time.

Implementing lean, REACH also reduced the time it spends collecting bedside information prior to transporting patients. Before, the verbal reports between hospital nurses and REACH's transport nurses had no structure. Hardcastle says, "We were experiencing a disconnect where the bedside nurse was reporting to us what she thought we needed to know—which was then often followed by a series of time-consuming questions that we actually needed to know." REACH standardized and sped up the process by creating a one-page flow sheet with essential information for each Level One category patient. When the sending facility has a Level One patient, for instance, it pulls and completes the flow sheet for that particular category. When REACH arrives, their staff has access to all of the essential criteria and requires little verbal reporting, thereby saving another three to five minutes.

REACH reduced more time waste by rethinking the way it handles infusions. Since the IV lines and other equipment to which a patient was tethered needed to stay at the sending facility, REACH had to transfer patients to its own equipment. Changing IV lines and inserting tubing was time-consuming, so the air ambulance company began supplying hospitals with REACH's transport infusion pump. REACH also provided training for the hospitals' staff members on how to use its equipment. Now, patients are ready for transport when the air ambulances arrive and REACH saves an additional 10 minutes from the process.

Lean transformation starts with changes in the ways people think about what they do, how they do it, and why it matters. REACH grasped the tenet early on and worked hard to get everyone involved. It improved communication and developed a series of successful training programs. By understanding the current reality of various activities, identifying an ideal state, and using process mapping to better structure its activities, REACH has been able to eliminate waste—in the form of potentially life-saving time. Using a systematic approach helps the company sustain its results.

## Marriott Towne Place Suites

The Novi, Michigan Marriott hotelier started its lean journey by sending one person, Operations Manager Heidi Lyman, to lean training. The one-woman lean "team" began applying lean principles by changing her vision of the hotel's ideal state. Lyman went from thinking that she must have daily interaction with guests to believing that she should rarely need to talk to guests. Staying away from customers may sound counterintuitive in a service-oriented environment, but she reasoned that if the hotel's processes were working, its staff members would be empowered to handle guests' needs. If she needed to intervene and help a customer, the process must have failed. This was a radical shift in thinking from the rest of the hospitality industry.

Lyman next focused on customer connections. Hotel guests are end-customers, but her new vision of the ideal state positioned employees as her direct customers. Lyman made it her responsibility to understand what each of her employees needed to serve guests in an efficient and effective manner.

Lastly, the hotel designed a responsive system. Lyman served the employees who, in turn, served the guests. She had to modify her role and processes to treat her employees as the customer. This was in line with the values of J.W. Marriott: "Take care of the associates and they will take care of the guests."

Lyman saw that the room-cleaning process needed more support and structure and appointed a cleaning staff team leader. Among the leader's many roles—which included getting laundry started earlier instead of waiting to collect all the dirty linens and towels, performing room inspections to ensure quality, coaching staff on key job skills—the most important function was serving as the key go-to resource. After restructuring the process, when members of the cleaning crew anticipated they would exceed the 50-minute standard cleaning time, they immediately called the team leader for help in completing the task in the allowed time. This ensured every room would be cleaned on time without adversely affecting the rest of the schedule. Small changes like this have made cleaning more efficient, effective, predictable, and reliable. By saving time through efficiencies, Marriott has been able to more than offset the costs of the new team leader position. By applying lean to its operations, the hotel's service score rose 10 points in less than one year. It went from the bottom half to the top 10% in its peer group across the nation.

Many other improvements at the hotel have been invisible to guests, but have nonetheless translated into added customer value and made the Marriott in Novi a shining example of lean service.

### Five Factors for Lean Service

1. Waste is hiding

2. Sweat the small stuff

3. It is hard to see the process

4. Design around and for the customer

5. Events are necessary

# 9

# The Transformation of One:
# Five Practices for Personal Lean

Lean primarily focuses on transformation at the organizational level and includes processes, collective thinking, decision-making, problem solving, and connections to the customer. But an organization is comprised of individuals, and individual behavior can play a major part in an organization's success. Individual performance is especially important at some organizations, such as schools and law firms. While the need for organizational-wide deployment of lean transformation should not be diminished, lean can help individuals (like you) be more effective.

People often ask, "I'm only one engineer (or a single supervisor, or a fill-in-the-blank). What impact can I make on my company's lean journey when I have so little power?" Assertively, individuals can lead up and try to influence those who wield more power. But they can also use lean to become a more skilled engineer (or a more effective supervisor or a better fill-in-the-blank). One transformed engineer will not turn a bad company into a good one, or a good company into a great one. But, the transformation will have a ripple effect. It will encourage others to join the journey. It will improve the engineer's ability to realize his or her goals. And (this is more important than it sounds), he or she will feel better at work.

What does it mean to apply lean on a personal level? An individual applying lean on a personal level is not going to do a kaizen, create a value stream map, or write standard work instructions. Nor is a person going to build a spaghetti diagram, put his or her desk into a U-shaped cell, or put an andon light above the desk chair. So what can a person do?

Many people start with Five S. They believe that it is relatively simple, and they like the idea of creating a cleaner personal work environment. By conducting Five S on his or her own work area, an individual can better appreciate the Five S process in the larger organization and can be more effective in supporting it. However, would a cleaner desk make anybody dramatically more effective or efficient? If so, then his or her work area must have been an environmental hazard. For most people, personal Five S is nice, but it does not embody transformation.

Personal lean delves beyond tools and influences how an individual thinks and how he or she approaches work—in much the same way as lean transforms an organization. To reiterate, "lean is not born from what we see; it is born from how we think." Five practices for personal effectiveness are explored in this chapter. Each practice begins with one of the fundamental lean principles covered in Chapter 1. Each practice is modified for application by an individual.

## PRACTICE ONE: ALWAYS WORK FOR THE CUSTOMER

The lean concept, "systematic waste elimination," focuses on the customer. It begins with the fundamental question, "What does my customer value?" and defines anything beyond the absolute minimum amount of resources needed to fulfill the customer's needs as waste.

Lean organizations look at every process, every activity, every dollar, and every minute as either providing customer value or not. What does this mean at the individual level? For starters, an individual needs to identify his or her customers. By focusing on the customer, a person can determine whether the daily work he or she performs adds value. Time should be looked at as an individual's most valuable resource. While time is money, money cannot buy more time. Once wasted, time cannot be reclaimed. Many years ago, a speaker at a conference made a profound and powerful comment: "Time is the currency of the 21st century. We spend time; we spend money. We invest time; we invest money. We budget time, save time, and waste time. What percentage of your time do you spend adding value?"

An individual's first priority should be maximizing value to the customer. Some persons might be bristling at this statement. This seems to run counter to the "me first" culture. Before thinking this is about charity, consider the notion of push versus pull. *Push* means that there is no demand for the resource, in this case an individual, but he or she produces anyway and essentially creates waste. *Pull* means that there is a demand, and a person can create value by filling a need. If an individual is providing value, he or she will be in demand, or pulled. If an individual creates waste, he or she must push and there is no fit. Those who are in demand are in a position to negotiate the rules, the conditions, and the price. Individuals should change the lens through which they view their relationship with others from, "What am I getting?" to, "How am I providing value?"

Sometimes a person is his own customer. Activities such as education, training, exercise, or reflection do not serve anyone else but the individual. But the person is still providing value— to himself. If an individual is not as likely to keep a commitment to himself as he is to others, then the person does not truly value commitment.

People despise the annual employee review ritual as much as doing their taxes. And why is that? Because most supervisors enter the process without a clear picture of what is valued. An employee generally wants to know the amount of (if any) raise he or she will be getting. Yet, most supervisors spend 30 minutes or more talking about a variety of issues. A supervisor could convey the information about the raise in 30 seconds. The employee does not see the value in the rest of the meeting and considers it wasted time. Imagine, however, if the supervisor provided actionable feedback. HR managers might be thinking this is exactly the point of reviews. But actionable feedback only works if both the employee and the supervisor truly value it and focus on delivering value. This rarely happens.

For another example, consider a visit to the doctor. A patient is the customer of the doctor. But the doctor is also the patient's customer. Doctors need accurate and relevant information from their patients to function. How well do you serve your doctor as a customer? Most doctors struggle with patients to get all of the information they need (as a customer of information) to do their job (as a supplier of treatment).

As outlined on the personal lean practices worksheet in Figure 9-1 (an electronic file of which is available for download at www.HitchhikersGuidetoLean.com), each day a person should begin by writing down who his or her customers will be for that

### Personal Lean Practices Worksheet

Practice 1: Always Work for Your Customer

| Today's Customers | Customer Wants | Delivered to Customer | Value-added Score |
|---|---|---|---|
| New employee on the team | Clarity on responsibilities | Instructions for job but not coaching | 33% |
| IT Department Manager | Needs update on next years' IT needs | Gave my personal view but not full team's | 50% |
| | | | |
| | | | |
| | | | |
| | | | |
| | | | |
| | | | |
| | | | |

(a)

Figure 9-1. Shown is the personal lean practices worksheet.

day. Next to that is written what the customers expect, or what they value. At the end of the day, or as a person completes tasks, what was actually delivered is written against the value. Dividing the delivered value by the desired value calculates the value-added percentage score. The score is subjective and for an individual's own use; inflation of the numbers is to be avoided. Brutal honesty will serve an individual well. Because the numbers are subjective, a person is not able to average the numbers or measure variations and an individual does not necessarily have to take action when his or her score is low. It is up to each person to know when to take corrective action. Individuals are simply focusing their attention on delivering daily value. In paying attention to customers an individual will naturally make changes to improve the scores.

At first, using the worksheet will be difficult. It may be hard to identify who is a customer. And, the value provided may not be obvious. But the payback will be immense because behaviors can be modified and prioritized based on what really makes a difference.

## PRACTICE TWO: PROBLEM SOLVING AT A RELATIONSHIP LEVEL

Relationships are critical to personal effectiveness, yet individuals give them much less attention than budget reviews, meeting schedules, and daily firefighting. Imagine what the result would be if the same rigor to problem solving at the organizational level was applied in relationships.

Fundamentally, the lean principle of "systematic problem solving" is about how individuals view problems. Problems must be brought to the surface and dealt with as quickly as possible. People must see problems as opportunities to move closer to the ideal state; they must dig deeper to get to the root causes.

A lean organization uses tools such as visual management and andon systems to spot and bring problems to the surface. It also uses five whys to solve problems and build a supportive infrastructure to focus attention in a timely manner. In contrast, most problem solving at the relationship level takes an opposite route. Individuals cover problems up or compensate for them. Often, an individual only deals with the symptom at the surface level because digging to the root cause is too uncomfortable.

To deal with relationship issues effectively, individuals must expose themselves and be vulnerable. Mechanisms such as placing blame, getting buy-in, and moving people to another spot on the organizational chart offer self-protection, but fail to fix the real problems.

Problem solving at the relationship level requires an individual to understand how to look at the root cause and symptoms. As an example, look at how you coordinate work with those around you. Too often you do not get what you need from people. Or, you get it, and it is either not up to par, late, or something other than what you requested. So, what do you do? In some cases, you simply stop working with the offending coworkers. At one company, the union leader and his management counterpart have not spoken to each other for years, and both seem quite comfortable with the arrangement (although the organization suffers).

When people can not rely on others to perform a task, they sometimes end up doing it themselves. In an extreme case, a maintenance supervisor had so little faith in his crew that he attended and led every machine maintenance activity, often with a team of skilled technicians standing around waiting for him. Solutions like these are rarely effective and often make things worse.

So, what should an individual do? At the root cause (which the five whys can help uncover), interpersonal problems among coworkers often occur when both persons have ineffective processes for managing conversations regarding commitments—especially breakdowns in commitment. Coordinated work is essentially a network of commitments. The more skilled an individual is at managing commitments, the more effective he or she can be at working with others and delivering results.

Coordinated work can begin to fail when coworkers do not verbalize the most important elements of a commitment, including: the expected result, what the output or product looks like, the time table for the commitment, why the commitment is important, identifying who will perform the action, identifying who is requesting the action, establishing a presumption of capability to perform the task, and identifying what else depends on the commitment. Sometimes individuals fail to review the elements of a commitment because they take them for granted; other times they simply ignore them. Either way, it can be a prescription for disaster.

Here is an example of how easy it is for commitments to break down. To monitor inventories at a plant, a supplier was called to find out the status of its latest production run and the planned delivery date. This was not uncommon, as the plant had not yet established stable systems. A call like this was usually a double check. The person at the supply company looked into the matter, but got sidetracked by other issues. He assumed the issue could wait until end of the business day. Unfortunately, the customer failed to communicate that his request was tied to another request—he needed to determine the support needed for weekend production. The supplier called back too late, and the customer was unable to plan for the plant's weekend needs.

How might the situation have been better handled? The natural reaction would have been to blame the supplier for not getting information back in a "timely" manner. But that would not have gotten to the root cause. Problem solving should focus on the process, so it must be determined how the process failed. The customer did not want to admit it, but he was the root cause when he failed to communicate that he needed the information by 3 p.m. to plan for the plant's weekend needs.

Instead of dealing with problems at the root-cause level, people often assign blame and choose damaging countermeasures that further deteriorate the relationship. Individuals should use systematic problem solving and the five whys to determine the true root cause. And this should not be done in a vacuum, but with the other person who experienced the lapse in communication.

On the personal lean practices worksheet in Figure 9-1(b), a block is included to help an individual monitor requests and

## Personal Lean Practices Worksheet

Practice 2: Problem-solving at a Relationship Level

| Commitment Request/Promise | Met / Unmet | Root Cause | Counter-measure |
|---|---|---|---|
| Information from peers for report to corporate | Unmet | Wasn't clear about reason for deadline | Created email template |
| Asked team to read an article for discussion | Met | | |
| | | | |
| | | | |
| | | | |
| | | | |
| | | | |

(b)

*Figure 9-1. (Continued)*

commitments and get to the root cause when a breakdown is experienced.

## PRACTICE THREE: PERSONAL LEARNING THROUGH PLAN/DO/CHECK/ACT

Plan/do/check/act (PDCA) is traditionally thought of as an organizational process for managing daily, monthly, and annual activities. But the tool also can be applied on a personal level to improve individual performance. This is the lean principle, "create a learning organization," which incorporates experimentation and reflection into every solution and improvement. In this case, the "organization" would be the individual.

There is one word that if used, and used with intent, will offer more power to an individual's personal learning than any other, and that word is *expect*. This word helps a person to develop a hypothesis, a theory that, if tested, will provide a wealth of information about what works and what does not. Here are some example expectations:

- If I leave 15 minutes early, I *expect* my trip to take 10 minutes less because of reduced traffic.
- If I appoint a timekeeper for a meeting, I *expect* that we will end on time.
- If I clearly state my objective in my discussion with my co-worker, I *expect* that we will not spiral into an argument.
- If I recheck my emails before I send them, I *expect* it will save time in the long run.

None of these expectations may turn out as planned. So, does frequently using the word "expect" set an individual up for disappointment? No, it sets the individual up for learning. Expectations establish educated guesses, or hypotheses. They are a person's best theories about how the world works, whether they apply to something mundane such as traffic patterns, or something complex such as human behavior. By testing each expectation, a person builds and internalizes knowledge of what works—and what does not work. This is how organizations that practice PDCA become more effective over time—and how an individual can too.

The application of plan/do/check/act may seem to take a lot of effort, but it really does not. A person starts by focusing on a topic or area that is of concern. For example, consider William. His job requires a lot of focused time on a few projects. However, it also requires a lot of fast-paced phone and e-mail communications as well as small activities. William is frustrated that small, detailed activities often interfere with his ability to focus on larger tasks. So, this is where he began his PDCA.

William started with an expectation—a detailed outline of his day. Keep in mind that this was an expectation, not an agenda or schedule to follow. As William went through the day, he checked (the "C" in PDCA) his actual events against his expected events and when there was a gap, he recorded why. He first noticed that long activities were behind schedule because of e-mail interruptions. He decided to disconnect from e-mail during the periods when he was performing larger tasks. William found the modification improved his ability to accomplish tasks. But, he noticed several activities that involved reviewing and responding to information that were either over- or under-scheduled. To compensate, he decided to review the amount of work before building his schedule. When William was able to generate a more accurate "expected" schedule, he noticed that he often was not able to get to critical tasks and had to jam them in at the end of the day. To fix this, he prioritized his activities and organized them into a sequenced plan. Over a period of two months of doing PDCA on his daily schedule, William changed many things about how he managed his time. The end result was an estimated 30–40% improvement in his productivity as measured by his output per day.

PDCA does not have to be time-consuming or complex. A simple "I expect" statement is sufficient. Figure 9-1(c) contains blocks that focus on plan and check. The *plan* is the activity to be performed or changed and its expectation, or hypothesis. The *check* is the actual result. It is recommended for individuals to maintain this record daily. Within a short period of time, payoffs will be seen.

## PRACTICE FOUR: MASTER WHAT YOU CAN CONTROL

Do you hear the phrase, "Things have been crazy lately," more than "Things have actually been pretty calm?" You are not alone. Is 21st-century life really more chaotic, or is everyone just less effective in dealing with it? Either way, people can not put aside work and job goals because life gets in the way or vice versa. Are you a victim of chaos, or a master of it? Do you focus on things beyond your control, or focus on those things you can control or influence?

To assume control, people do not necessarily need to eliminate the whirlwind of activity around them. Chaos is often ex-

## Personal Lean Practices Worksheet

Practice 3: Personal Learning Through Plan/Do/Check/Act

| PLAN : Action | PLAN: Expectation | CHECK: Actual Result from Action |
|---|---|---|
| Expanded staff meeting to include key internal suppliers | Faster response time on key requests | Will be measuring response time on IT requests and HR requests |
| Unplug network during report writing | Increase productivity 50% | Measure minutes per page—baseline is 10 |
| | | |
| | | |
| | | |
| | | |
| | | |
| | | |

(c)

*Figure 9-1. (Continued)*

ternally driven and beyond an individual's control. The focus should be on what can be controlled. The lean principle at play here is "establish high agreement of what and how." When applied to groups and organizations, the principle refers to establishing a common purpose, goal, method, and sequence among the larger group. Of course, this part of the principle is irrelevant in the context of personal lean. However, the principle also focuses on eliminating variation in the process. By eliminating variation, individuals can create more predictable outcomes and a more stable base on which to improve.

Individuals can create standardization and stability through structured work by first identifying the sources of variation and disruption that prevent personal efficiency. There are some simple countermeasures that can be deployed, but an individual needs to first recognize the value in questioning his or her own effectiveness. Arriving at the answers will help an individual determine a logical path to the countermeasures. Once an individual understands the issue, he or she will know which tools to apply for the best solution. Here are the specific questions that should be asked.

1. *What repetitive issues do you encounter that cause significant disruption due to their urgency and intrusion?* The answer will depend on the type of work you engage in. It will also depend on whether advance warning is needed to head off the intrusion, or whether you need to be aware of the damage caused by the disruptions after the fact. As an example, if you need to interrupt your work so that you can run to the office store when you run out of key supplies, a kanban system would let you know of your needs in advance. Solutions that focus on programmed responses to interruptions might include pre-arranged backup resources or templates for making the responses less intrusive. By controlling or eliminating repetitive disruptions, a person can focus on what *should* be done versus what *needs* to be done.

2. *What processes or areas can quickly get you in trouble? And what can you check to anticipate meltdowns before they become a problem?* Consider this your work's health checkup or routine maintenance. You should not wait until a treatable ailment jeopardizes your health, right? And, car owners should check their automobile's belts, oil level, and seals to help prevent their engines from failing in the middle of the highway. Likewise, instead of waiting to find out that your team has shipped defects, test your quality control to make sure it is working. Instead of waiting to find out you are late on meeting commitments, check the

oldest date on your to-do list or inbox. Instead of waiting for your computer to crash, check the virus scanning software or the disk volume. You do not need to develop a long maintenance list. But you do need to cover the essentials to ward off problems.

3. *What conversations, searches, or reviews provide you with critical information before you need it?* Depending on what you do, your information source might be research, a customer, or a trusted individual who is connected to your business. When information arrives too late it is, well, too late. You need to be proactive and seek out the information that will be most beneficial for your job.

Once an individual has asked the above questions and figured out ways to anticipate and avoid intrusions, he or she then needs to consider how to respond to the inevitable variation and chaos. In contrast to other animals, humans have the freedom, intellect, and will to make calculated choices. If someone cuts in front of you on the highway, you can choose to tailgate and flash your lights, or you can choose to back off to a safe distance. Effective individuals focus on issues they can control or influence. (In other words, back off!) For example, there are many reasons why someone might show up late to work one day. A traffic accident would generally be outside anyone's control, so focusing on it by complaining, venting, or redirecting would be futile. If, however, someone left his house earlier for work, he or she would have control over that factor.

Focusing on customers who change their minds leads to frustration. But by designing a value-delivery system that accommodates customers who change their minds, an individual can be back in control and able to respond effectively to the chaos. Similarly, instead of focusing on an inadequate budget, someone could focus on prioritizing, making decisions, and leveraging the budget.

So how can individuals turn mastering what they can control into daily practice? In Figure 9-1(d) there is a space provided

Personal Lean Practices Worksheet

Practice 4: Master of What You Can Control

| Control Point (What Can be Done Proactively?) | OK (No Action) | Not OK (Action Taken) |
|---|---|---|
| Check for oldest date of emails in inbox to ensure requests are being met on time | | 4 emails over 1 month old—added color code for emails over two weeks old to highlight their age |
| Ask one employee (each day) if they are getting the support they need to do their job | OK | |
| | | |
| | | |
| | | |
| | | |
| | | |
| | | |

Practice 5: See More With Your Own Eyes
Circle the activity(ies) on Figures 9-1a-d wherein you used direct observation

(d)

*Figure 9-1. (Continued)*

for daily control point standardization. On this section of the worksheet, an individual refers to the questions and information above and then determines the things that need to be accomplished.

## PRACTICE FIVE: SEE MORE WITH YOUR OWN EYES

Practice Five has more to do with how an individual performs the four. It relates to the lean principle of "directly observe work as activities, connections and flows." Most specifically, it is about direct observation, or using your own eyes to collect information for solving problems, making decisions, or improving work.

Advocating seeing things with your own eyes does not mean to imply that you should not trust anyone. This is simply not true, and it is a disheartening attitude. But seeing things with your own eyes offers, quite simply, understanding. A person may think he or she knows all the factors affecting a decision or a process, but the only way to really know is by checking. By directly observing the processes, practices, and areas that most specifically affect your work and your world, you will become a better student of those areas. By studying how things really work, a person gains knowledge over time that facilitates more effective decisions. Understanding the underlying processes and how they really work is invaluable information and impossible to find in any book.

To raise an individual's awareness of the role direct observation plays in decision making, the elements completed using direct observation are circled on the other four sections of the personal lean practices worksheet (Figures 9-1[a–d]). By doing this daily, and reviewing the results, an individual should begin applying the practice more often.

Building lean into personal practices can help a person work more effectively. And, by applying lean to work, an individual can become an effective teacher and leader to help others also apply lean.

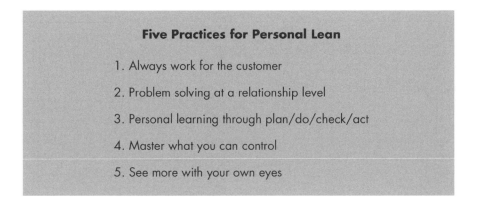

**Five Practices for Personal Lean**

1. Always work for the customer

2. Problem solving at a relationship level

3. Personal learning through plan/do/check/act

4. Master what you can control

5. See more with your own eyes

# 10

## Conversations from the Road

Oh, the people you meet when you travel on a journey. On our lean journey, we have met many great people and many effective leaders. In this chapter, five such leaders relate their stories. Each has a different role, different perspective, and a different challenge, but all have delivered results.

The leaders were asked a set of identical questions regarding their lean journeys. Their varied responses are educational and inspirational—we learned from these leaders, and we hope you will too. We also hope you will take the questions we asked and ask them of other leaders. Or, ask them of yourself — you may be suprised at how valuable your own experiences are for learning.

## ROBERT FINN
## RSR CORPORATION

Robert Finn is the President and CEO of RSR Corporation, a leading, privately held, U.S.-based lead smelter that recycles lead acid batteries and other lead-bearing materials to produce pure lead and a complete line of calcium and antimonial lead alloys. RSR operates three plants: California, New York, and Indiana; and is headquartered in Dallas. The lean journey started in all three plants at approximately the same time after leaders commissioned independent lean assessments and basic lean training for the management groups. This interview relates his experiences.

*Question*: "How has your lean journey unfolded so far?"

*Finn*: "Pathetically slow—of course, 'slow' is a relative term. I am not the most patient person at times. I had expected to see widespread significant gains much quicker than we did. However, I now recognize that this will be a slower journey than I had hoped. We have had some significant improvement with one plant setting new productivity and profitability standards, but truly I expected more by now. Since we started on our lean journey our accomplishments have been, for the most part, small. But we are building on the small achievements and in the near future we expect widespread larger gains."

*Question*: "What has been your greatest victory?"

*Finn*: "With little effort we were able to get the majority of the workforce to agree that we needed to change our culture to compete in our markets on a worldwide basis. We decided that if a culture change was what we truly needed we would need to convince our most pragmatic individuals right out of the box; without their wholehearted support there was no way we would succeed. Once we got them convinced, the majority of the workforce followed. This was particularly satisfying because the lean assessments of the plants indicated that, although the company had a willing workforce, it was also a skeptical workforce. We still have pockets of the organization that have not recognized the need, but this is a small percentage of the workforce and dwindling. I am not saying that we have changed the culture; I am saying the 'need' to change is recognized and accepted by most of the company. The first step in any change initiative is to recognize the need. I guess we are doing okay."

*Question*: "What has been your greatest failure or struggle?"

*Finn*: "There are actually two. First, we completely underestimated the length of time it would take to change the culture. In our factories our employees average 13 years of service; 13 years of old habits are not going to change in 24 months. We are in a harsh and traditional industry that has not ever really focused on a structured continuous improvement approach. We were, and still are to a large degree, deficient in our basic continuous improvement skills. I think a lot of employee involvement programs, like suggestion programs, fail because we ask employees to contribute but don't teach them how to go about it. Second, I focused most of my day-to-day involvement at the managerial level and failed to establish a solid connection to the shop floor. The responsibility of a leader is to exhibit the behaviors you would like to see in your organization. I did not have the mechanisms and structure to make it happen. This mistake probably cost us at least a year in developmental changes. Additionally, we spent countless hours training the shop-floor employees, but failed to establish empowered core teams with accountability. The establishment of a small work group structure would have helped. It is important to look at the organization and its operating structure. Whatever initiatives you pursue, they need to be compatible with your operating structure."

*Question*: "What result has most surprised you?"

*Finn*: "My biggest surprise was that highly educated professionals had difficulty grasping and adopting the concepts of lean manufacturing. The people on the shop floor and the clerk in the office were easier to develop into lean thinkers; they were more willing to embrace the concepts. This may be because of the nature of our business, the history of our organization, or because we did not work hard enough to build creative tension within their ranks. Whatever the reason, it was a surprise. I expected that the simple mandate to these professionals that "lean is not optional," combined with some training and exposure, would be sufficient. It wasn't. I had to make some difficult decisions to make sure the right people were in the right seats; in some cases, this called for the removal of people from the company. Regardless, it has been very encouraging, and a pleasant surprise, to see shop-floor employees take an active role in lean transformation and not just act as passive bystanders providing lip service."

*Question*: "How have you deployed lean tools throughout the organization?"

*Finn*: "We introduced the principles of lean thinking using an airplane factory simulation in a lab environment. Every employee was required to attend. Building on the airplane simulation, we introduced monthly lean learning labs that focused on a particular lean principle and tool. The participants in the labs were required to practice on the shop floor and then reflect on the results. One major issue was how to communicate to employees what good looked like. So, we showed them by taking them to Toyota for facility tours. This has proven to be an eye-opening experience for employees. They now see the potential of lean.

"We used independent lean assessments of our plants to help us assess the gap between where we were versus where we would like to be in the future. It was clear that we needed to completely understand our current reality before we could design our lean implementation plan. What was interesting was the assessments did not really uncover much of what we didn't already know. What it did uncover was that, as an organization, we didn't have a common understanding of the complete picture. Each of us had pieces and we had no focused vision to compare our reality against."

*Question*: "How do you know if the lean culture is catching on and becoming sustainable?"

*Finn*: "From my perspective, the culture shift is measured by the quality of the improvements. Initially, we saw some individuals seeming to embrace lean as a method to further their own agendas, primarily moving accountability and responsibility from their areas into another's. Eventually we resolved those issues through the traditional methods. The groups that routinely get it as it pertains to lean are the ones who understand how a process change in their areas can benefit other areas as well.

"We are also beginning to see some shared benefit from plant to plant, not just within the plants. It was probably smart that, considering our plants are practically identical in their operations, we started a lean learning lab in a different area in each plant. This gave us three areas in which to test, learn, and share. This should facilitate an effective and efficient expansion in the plants using our lessons learned. Another measure of any real cultural change is the sustainability of the lean initiatives in the absence of management pushing and prodding. I think we could change the management team in two of our plants and the lean journey would continue with minimal interference. In one plant we did lose our management team. We had to intervene and are now putting significant effort into halting the backslide."

*Question*: "What would you do differently if you could start over?"

*Finn*: "I would spend 90% of all training and interactions on the shop-floor employees and their immediate supervisors. The shop-floor level is where the money will be made. Now that we are finally working with these employees I am routinely impressed with the quality and sincerity of the observations made by this group."

*Question*: "What have you changed about how you do your own work?"

*Finn*: "It is more systematic, purpose-driven, and deliberate. My focus is now more on the 'why' versus the 'who.' While visiting our facilities I unconsciously find myself conducting waste walks, examining scorecards, and evaluating the quality of the lean effort. I tend to preach less, coach more, and always try to provide a vision for the future. This has not been an easy transition for me. I thought I was a pretty good 21st-century leader until I realized there were still many skills and traits I needed to develop to be a true lean leader. I think the people in my organization are seeing a difference and are responding."

*Question*: "What are your next steps? Where will you go next on your lean journey?"

*Finn*: "We will continue to focus on developing the shop-floor-level employees or have them develop us; it goes both ways. We will stress the quality of actions, not the numbers or dollars; they will follow. It is the many small improvements that lead to a significant gain. It is fixing the small day-to-day problems so they do not become big problems. The dollars are important, but the focus needs to be on the activities and not just the dollars. I think we also need to do a better job of assuring that every activity, every project, every new skill developed, and every dollar invested is obviously and measurably aligned and connected to the goals of the organization. We should never be doing anything where we cannot make the connection."

## SHAWN PATTERSON
## DTE ENERGY

This interview explores the lean journey of Shawn Patterson who was the founding Director of the Operating System Strategy Group at DTE Energy. His group was responsible for supporting the development and deployment of the DTE Energy operating system. The group facilitated a wide range of activities including training, coaching, projects, and assessment. He continues on with DTE Energy in an operational leadership role, deploying the operating system for the organization.

*Question*: "How has your lean journey unfolded so far?"

*Patterson*: "It has been far slower than I expected. Although a great deal of progress has been made, it has been a much longer journey than I would have expected. The cultural part of the change has been much more challenging than the systems part. It is pretty easy to teach the tools of lean and six sigma. But it is far more difficult to convince people that behaviors need to change—and that these changes need to start with them. Leaders are the most difficult group to impact; leadership hubris can be strong among senior-level managers.

"As we look back, we have done a decent job of following the transformation roadmap. It is crucial for the lean transformation journey."

*Question*: "What has been your greatest victory?"

*Patterson*: "The greatest victory has been getting senior leaders to invest their time and money in the program. Deciding to become a lean organization is as much a strategic decision as deciding to expand into a new market. It requires retooling the skills of an organization, redefining organizational structures, and committing resources and time. Too many companies see lean as a security blanket for their board of directors or investors. It looks good to say that they have a lean program.

I am proud to say that at DTE Energy we have broken through and have tangible evidence that our leadership is serious about making lean transformation work.

"We have a commitment to training, resource allocation, and leadership time. Leaders are now seeing the gap between where the collective organizational skills are and where they need to be in the future. They are encouraging employees to dig deeper to understand problems and develop solutions. We are turning the corner. It has been a long process, but it is paying off."

*Question*: "What has been your greatest failure or struggle?"

*Patterson*: "The greatest failure was not being conscious of the cultural struggles encountered in transforming the organization. In hindsight, I would have surrounded myself with the very best change management specialists from the get go. I think this is an area that still does not have a great many solutions, but it is the next frontier in making lean transformation faster and more sustainable."

*Question*: "What result has most surprised you?"

*Patterson*: "What has been most surprising is the power that one key leader can bring. We were fortuitous to have a strong six sigma leader come to DTE Energy to lead one of our business units. The influence that he has had on his peers has been incredible. He has produced compelling results that the executive leaders use as case examples across the organization. He has been determined to set up an organizational structure to support lean and six sigma and has encouraged his peers to do the same. I know that we would not be where we are if it were not for this leader.

"As I said in answering the previous question, deciding to become a lean organization is a strategic choice. It requires retooling the organization. It requires strong internal change leaders and at least one executive champion who is not only passionate, but also truly knows what a good lean program looks like.

"In retrospect, I have also been amazed at the results that we have produced by applying lean and six sigma tools. I would have thought $150 million in improvements for an organization with $1.8 billion in Operations & Maintenance would have been impossible. We have achieved great results but I still feel we could be doing so much more."

*Question*: "How have you deployed lean tools throughout the organization?"

*Patterson*: "We have used a number of approaches. First, we have established a Black Belt program to train strong internal change leaders whose full-time responsibility is to work on key projects and mentor others. We also have a specialist program that is intended to provide employees with a general understanding of lean and six sigma tools.

"For the bulk of the organization, lean is learned through application. We have employees participate in kaizens, waste walks, corrective action record (CAR) teams, etc. Through repetition, they learn the basic tools and begin to use them in their work environments. Over the last five years, employees have gone from not knowing what the word "kaizen" even meant to using it in their everyday vocabulary. It takes time, but it is the only way to get the entire organization involved, in my opinion."

*Question*: "How do you know if the lean culture is catching on and becoming sustainable?"

*Patterson*: "The biggest indicator to me is that our leadership has been clear in communicating that those who can lead change through use of the operating system will be the ones who will assume higher levels of responsibility. If you cannot lead change using the lean tools, you will not move on. This has created an expectation that has mid-level leaders seeking to improve their skills."

*Question*: "What would you have done differently if you could start over?"

*Patterson*: "In addition to paying more attention to the challenges of change management, I would advocate hiring a senior line leader who is a lean expert."

*Question*: "What have you changed about how you do your own work?"

*Patterson*: "I have learned to be far more collaborative in my work as an internal consultant. I came to the company somewhat headstrong, believing that leaders would inherently see the value in what I could offer. I have learned the transformation needs to be owned by leaders. Thus my role needs to be one of leading them down a path of enlightenment through benchmarking, teaching, sending articles, sharing case studies, lining up guest speakers, etc.

"I have also learned that I need to be more collaborative with other internal support organizations. Communications, organizational development, finance, and others really need to be on board to move forward in a collective manner. I failed to enroll these areas in the beginning and it led to many delays."

*Question*: "What are your next steps? Where will you go next on your lean journey?"

*Patterson*: "We are now working on our Phase II implementation plan. We are clearly documenting where we are and where we need to go over the next 18–24 months, again using the transformation roadmap as the underpinning structure.

"I have moved into a line role and am in a stronger place of advocacy. I am working to improve the skills of my managers and build the right support organization within our business unit. Finally, I am trying to provide a clearer set of priorities (Hoshin planning) and expectations (behaviors) for my direct reports. I enjoy driving change through direct authority versus lobbying as an internal lean consultant."

## DENNIS PAWLEY
## CHRYSLER CORPORATION

The following is an interview with Dennis Pawley who was Executive Vice President of Manufacturing and Labor Relations at Chrysler Corporation during Chrysler's stellar run of performance leading up to the creation of DaimlerChrysler. He is credited with leading the creation and deployment of the Chrysler operating system (COS) through an almost 90,000-person-strong organization. COS is the vehicle being used to close the gap from the company's current state to its vision. Dennis Pawley is one of the most respected leaders in the automotive industry. This interview relates his experiences along the lean journey at Chrysler. Dennis is currently the CEO of Pawley Enterprises (Farmington Hills, MI) and Partner at the Lean Learning Center (Novi, MI).

*Question:* "What was your greatest victory on the lean journey?"

*Pawley:* "There are a lot of them but I think the greatest was convincing higher-level leaders at vice president and plant manager levels that they bore more responsibility in teaching people how to think and operate differently than they ever had before. They had more leadership responsibilities under these new efforts than the technical responsibilities of how to build a vehicle, and this required a big leap for many people. Seeing that change happen with 70% of the leaders was the most significant victory."

*Question:* "What was your greatest failure or struggle?"

*Pawley:* "It was to convince the people above me and equal to me in the corporation that they should take the training themselves and understand at the same level of depth that I did, rather than just voice it and support it. The problem was that I needed to make the leaders in the organization realize that this was more than a small "m"anufacturing, four-walls-of-the-plant initiative. It was a big "M"anufacturing initiative that would touch everything—how we design, build, sell and service our vehicles—to truly make it successful and compete in the market."

*Question:* "What result has most surprised you?"

*Pawley:* "It completely redefined the measurement and definition of what a plant manager did, along with their staffs all the way down to the front-line supervisor. Their jobs were completely different. We redefined the job responsibilities and how individuals think about and do those jobs. And we changed how we measured and evaluated people with that change. Under the old measurement system, many people were not doing a good job. And some people that were only average in the old system became shining stars when the evaluation system changed to reflect the new direction. Some of those who were shining stars in the old system were now incapable in the new system. They could not make the change. This surprise of where people shook out reflects a most important lesson: 'if you can't teach, you can't lead.'"

*Question:* "How were lean tools deployed throughout the organization?"

*Pawley:* "Cascade teaching was our approach—leaders teach leaders all the way down the organization. I would teach the first class to my vice presidents. They would have to learn it, because they had to turn right around and teach their direct reports. And then they had to teach, and so on. This gave me the ability to test the understanding of each level of the organization. And, based on how they were learning and teaching, I could see who was capable of applying this and who was not."

*Question:* "How did you know the lean culture was catching on and becoming sustainable?"

*Pawley:* "The only way I could really know was by walking the floor and asking questions and then listening to the answers. I was not asking questions that would lead to reactive actions by people. The questions asked were proactive—about the process and how it created results. In listening to the answers I got back I was able to assess if people were changing their thinking about the work. This was the only way I could do it. You can not do it by handing out a questionnaire or survey."

*Question:* "What would you do differently if you could start over?"

*Pawley:* "We started out teaching the tools of lean, and I would have instead concentrated more on finding ways to teach lean thinking. It got so people would know the tools and they could even use them effectively. But without having a basic understanding of what it means to think differently behind the tools, lean could not go as far as it had to. If I had done that, it would have been different."

*Question:* "What did you change about how you did your own work?"

*Pawley:* "The first three years in that job, I was a pretty traditional manufacturing-type guy. I would visit the plants, take the housekeeping tour, listen to safety reports, kick the tires, chew some people out, and leave. Then I changed how I went into the organization. I became a lean role model, teaching people how they needed to think and act. I went from being 80% reactive to what happened and 20% proactive, to being 80% proactive and 20% reactive. That was a big change."

*Question:* "What are your next steps? Where will you go next on your lean journey?"

*Pawley:* "I learned in my 10 years at Chrysler how hard it is to take minds that are like steel traps and begin to pry them open; it is a tough, tough task. When trying to do that across all of American industry, not just one company, the change may just not happen soon enough. My involvement in the Lean Learning Center will help companies move forward from where they are, keeping industry alive. I will continue to spend time with companies that need to change today, but from my perspective the real solution is working with universities and the students, which is why I am spending my time and money there. A new type of thinking must be instilled in the leaders of the future so they can apply lean on day one on the job to carry on the journey."

Note: Dennis Pawley has funded and founded the Pawley Institute at Oakland University (Rochester, MI), which is dedicated to advancing the education of lean in undergraduate and graduate studies.

# ROBERT SMILLIE
# NEMAK CORPORATION

Robert Smillie is Vice President of Nemak Corporation and is responsible for its Canadian operations. Nemak is a global organization and part of the Alfa Group, which is headquartered in Monterrey, Mexico. Nemak of Canada specializes in the production of aluminum cylinder heads and engine-block castings for the worldwide automotive and truck industry. One of the plants Bob is responsible for, Windsor Aluminum, was a Shingo Award finalist in 2004. Bob spent the first 34 years of his career with Ford Motor Company in a variety of senior management positions. The last five years he has led Nemak of Canada operations. Bob was also a recipient of the Shingo Award in 1996, and is a certified Shingo Award examiner. The following interview conveys his experiences along the lean journey at Nemak.

*Question:* "How has your lean journey unfolded so far?"

*Smillie:* "Remarkably well. It is the primary reason why I have stayed in the automotive business so long. Lean continues to expose new and exciting opportunities in our operations. It has really helped us increase productivity and it has been especially helpful in improving customer satisfaction. Even after five years at Nemak, and with many successes, I believe we are just beginning to scratch the surface of what is possible."

*Question:* "What has been your greatest victory so far?"

*Smillie:* "We have secured new work in Canada in an extremely competitive market. Also particularly gratifying is our working relationship with our union and staff to get everybody feeling that they are part owners of the business. We continually focus our efforts on reinforcing their learning around common and clearly understood goals and objectives. Simply put, 'Everybody must get it.' In 1995, my manager and I would spend every Friday afternoon reviewing chapters of lean books and articles. I would explain what I thought the chapter meant to our organization and we would then build on that conversation for clarification, application, and continuing education. The message I would like to pass on from this learning experience is, 'Benchmark and learn from the best. You will know success when others knock on your door wanting to learn from you and your organization.'"

*Question:* "What has been your greatest failure or struggle?"

*Smillie:* "When I first visited Toyota in 1983, their senior leadership told me that the U.S. automotive industry would never successfully implement lean because they did not have the patience and they would not give it the time to mature. They were right. We sacrificed long-term growth and stability for short-term results. The financial community within our industry continues to push and pressure for immediate results without first stabilizing the organization and its processes. Even our traditional financial accounting systems are often in conflict with lean systems. My recommendation is to get the financial community onboard from the very beginning. They can help identify and eliminate roadblocks before they become major issues."

*Question:* "What results most surprised you?"

*Smillie:* "I don't think much surprised me. Delighted is probably a better description. I am delighted that the majority of our hourly workforce wants to contribute and succeed in improving productivity and quality. They know improvements in productivity could result in fewer jobs. But our emphasis is on attracting new work by being competitive. If we can earn new work, the jobs will follow. Since I consider quality to be a given and cost reduction a result, I am delighted to see the emphasis focused on process improvements and our customers. I am also delighted that lean has prompted and promoted the sharing of best practices between our customers and our suppliers. This has significantly improved customer relations. Success breeds excitement and today we are flying high. We have traction."

*Question:* "How have you developed lean tools throughout the organization?"

*Smillie:* "It has not been without many false starts. We tried to implement lean tools without first understanding their purpose and without knowing how the tools interrelate. We had to stop and take a break. We had to step back, clarify our vision, and re-baptize the organization. We then spread the new vision throughout the organization using lean thinking to drive the lean application. Effective policy deployment was the mechanism that provided the compass for our lean journey and it has been our salvation. One caution is that policy deployment must be kept simple and understood by all."

*Question:* "How do you know if the lean culture is catching on and becoming sustainable?"

*Smillie:* "We know the culture is catching on and is stable and sustainable because we do not change our objectives year after year. We are currently working on next year's objectives. We only have five, and four of those are a carryover from prior years. No one is confused about what is expected or what he or she should be working on to satisfy what is expected." *(Authors note: This was the most surprising and enlightening comment received in response to this question.)*

*Question:* "What would you do differently if you could start over?"

*Smillie:* "No banners, pendants, signs, or slogans. I would never do it again. It is too fake. Also I would ensure that I had a 'top-down' and 'bottom-up' development plan implemented concurrently. We 'educated' our management, but we 'developed' the shop floor. What happens is the shop floor matures and gets ahead of management and then management is guarded and fearful of involvement because of possible embarrassment. Another mistake we made was not fully engaging middle management. We thought they would take the lean concepts and run. The problem is we never gave them the total training and management support they needed."

*Question:* "What has changed about how you do your own work?"

*Smillie:* "What has not changed is an easier question to answer, but a couple of things do stand out. I used to simply demand that my team do their job. This was pretty simple. But now I ensure they clearly understand and agree to the common goals and objectives. I give them the skills and tools and then hold them accountable to deliver on their objectives. This is far more difficult. Also, senior leadership must be visible and teaching on the shop floor. People need to see who is running the business. This does not constitute just walking around and shaking hands. Leaders need to observe the work, assess performance, and provide direction as needed while on the floor. Each senior leader is required to understand lean principles well enough to teach and champion one of the lean elements."

*Question:* "What are your next steps?"

*Smillie:* "We are going global with the Nemak operating system. We want to standardize and use a common operating system across all our plants worldwide. Common metrics with common definitions and formulas will be instituted throughout all the business units. Beyond the obvious benefits, this will also establish an internal benchmarking process for our organization. Also, we need to develop and implement additional mechanisms to empower our people even more. I believe we have just begun to tap the potential of our workforce, which is where the true power of lean manufacturing lies. We can all go to the same lean workshops. We can all read the hundreds of text books written on lean principles. But as I have said before, 'It is the people who truly make the difference.'"

## JOHN SMITH
## ROSS CONTROLS

The following interview is with John G. Smith, Chief Operating Officer and Senior Vice President of Ross Controls. John has more than 30 years experience in manufacturing. His career began in the area of finance, where he served in various management positions including Chief Financial Officer. He was promoted to Operations in 2000 where is he is involved with implementation and deployment of lean principles and practices. As part of the journey, John has successfully developed a lean culture at Ross. He has led the transformation of many processes in the company's manufacturing facilities in Michigan (a union environment) and Georgia (a non-union environment). This interview relates his experiences along the way.

*Question:* "How has your lean journey unfolded so far?"

*Smith:* "Our lean journey has been very successful. Over the past two years we have taken substantial dollars out of our inventory. Better yet, we have been able to change the mix of inventory from a heavily weighted finished goods and work-in-process (WIP) inventory to a mix favoring raw materials and WIP. This reduces cost and allows for more flexibility, which is important in our business. We are much more dependent on throughput rather than the high cost of trying to determine which products should be on the shelf.

"Because our employees have learned from their lean education the value of waste elimination and the importance of customer service, they understand the value of improving throughput. More importantly, they are really beginning to understand the key to waste elimination is in process improvements and standardization of process and procedure.

"Of course, like all journeys, we encounter a fork in the road occasionally. Sometimes we have been fortunate and taken the correct way and other times we have taken the less favorable way. When we do take off in the wrong direction, we take advantage of the trip and do a little sightseeing and try to learn from the experience."

*Question:* "What has been your greatest victory?"

*Smith:* "It is hard to imagine victory with lean. Since lean is a journey and not a destination, you cannot have victory over it but maybe small victories within it. To not be victorious implies defeat. Defeat is not an option. One can only hope to enjoy the high points and learn from the low as we travel along the winding path of lean. High points come when you see employees' eyes light up when they recognize the meaning of a lesson on lean or when they apply the rules, tools and principles of lean without needing encouragement from others. The greatest satisfaction comes from seeing the culture of your organization change: seeing people who in the past have approached life with a jaded view begin to smile and feel self-worth as they implement an idea that in the past would have landed on deaf ears; seeing those who have suffered through life always being right realize the value of a team member's contribution; or when a person uses their newfound knowledge to teach others the value and rewards of improvement over the unrewarding status quo. Lean offers everyone in the organization a reason to be successful in whatever they do."

*Question:* "What has been your greatest failure or struggle?"

*Smith:* "Failure is not an option. But yes, there are many struggles on this journey. How can you possibly learn if you do not make mistakes? I do not think I could list all of the mistakes I have made on this journey. However, it is important to understand that with lean we must encourage others to take chances and make improvements they feel are possible. If it works we have made progress, if it does not work we reflect on why it did not work and learn from our mistake. I view mistakes as good learning experiences and opportunities to make change. It is the famous two steps forward and one step back. Sometimes it may be two back and one forward, for example, a kaizen that had such potential but rendered only minimum results or the constant battle of keeping others interested in the true value of lean. We do not have the luxury of having someone dedicated to lean but rather work toward everyone seeing the value of lean. My greatest struggle is consistency. It is so easy to get caught up in the day to day of the business with all the issues we must deal with. All of a sudden you realize it has been a week or two since you have spent time teaching."

*Question:* "What result has most surprised you?"

*Smith:* "I don't know if I could identify a single result that has surprised me the most but I can say that I am blown away at how little changes can have big impacts on the business. It is understandable why Toyota concentrates on many small changes rather than on one big home run. We have seen small changes made by one person encourage a small change by another person. The infectious idea of one person making a small change, which in turn causes a change in behavior of another person, is remarkable."

*Question:* "How have you deployed lean tools throughout the organization?"

*Smith:* "We have used many of the tools provided by lean. I have found that using the tools is relatively easy. People can learn the tools and understand the benefit of most of them with proper instruction/education. The work environment is cleaner and more organized. People understand the need to eliminate waste and, for the most part, they recognize that waste elimination is essential for the company to be competitive in today's market. However, people recognize that using the tools alone is not enough to get the job done. A change in behavior and thinking is required to make real improvement. The key to real change lies within the rules and principles of lean: high agreement . . . what is it?, how do you reach it?, and how do you apply it?; and systematic problem-solving . . . who does it?, and how do you make it part of everyone's day-to-day thinking? Yes, we do use the tools and for sure they are a required part of lean, but I don't believe that the tools will get the job done. Like many people we erred on the side of implementing tools when we first began. It became apparent very quickly that if we were going to be successful with lean we needed to concentrate on changing the way people think about what we do. To change the way people think, we recognized the need to change the very basis of how they think and act each day, which meant we needed rules and principles to guide us."

*Question:* "How do you know if the lean culture is catching on and becoming sustainable?"

*Smith:* "This is an interesting question. There is no doubt that the company's culture has changed. However, there is also no doubt that the more it changes the more we see the need to change it more. It becomes obvious why this is called a journey. We have seen substantial improvement in the culture; people who in the past have been written off have become fantastic employees and real contributors. That is culture change. We have seen people, or groups, who in the past would not work together now seeking advice and help from each other. That is culture change. We have seen some of the company nay sayers turn around and actually begin to sing a little praise for what lean is and what it has done for the company. That is culture change.

"Sustainable? Yes, I think it has become sustainable. But, I also believe it could slip away over time if not held out as being important to the business and supported with the relentless effort of company leadership. The need for change and continuous improvement has become a part of the culture. It has become a sustainable part of the way we think."

*Question:* "What would you do differently if you could start over?"

*Smith:* "We started by trying to teach people the tools. After a couple of months of effort we realized people were not becoming involved and the tools alone were not the answer. After shifting our attitude of what was important, we began to teach employees why they needed to change their thinking. We used the rules and principles of lean everywhere possible and things began to change in the company. Would I do it differently if I were starting over? Of course, but only because hindsight is 20/20. This was a mistake for us but it was not devastating. We needed the tools, but we needed the principles of lean more. We needed to teach our employees 'how' to make change and 'why' it was not threatening to them. Lean is all about learning. The important thing is to start. Regardless of where you start, you will make a change in the approach as time moves on as you determine the most important area of need in your particular organization."

*Question:* "What have you changed about how you do your own work?"

*Smith:* "I have but one job—to educate and promote others. No one person is perfect but a team can be. I have always believed my job was to promote others but lean has taught me that this can only be achieved through leadership."

*Question:* "What are your next steps? Where will you go next on your lean journey?"

*Smith:* "We started our lean journey in manufacturing. Everyone in our company has seen the benefits and the changes there. Recently we introduced our corporate group to lean. Training and education have taken place and we held our first kaizen event with this group. The kaizen included engineering, marketing, communications, legal and finance. Our next step is to expand the lean culture into the G & A groups of the company.

"My summary thoughts are this—it has become very clear to us that lean is a way of life. It is also clear that regardless of the number of changes we make, we see the need for more. Improvement is fun. One or two improvements uncover the need for other improvements. Lean is like a pebble (improvement) pitched softly into a still pond (the work environment). It creates ripples (more improvements) that grow larger (viewable) and larger into each other."

# Index

# W